VICTORY OVER FEAR AND WORRY

DR. ROBERT A. RUSSELL

Audio Enlightenment Press

Giving Voice to the Wisdom of the Ages

Printed in the United States of America

First Printing, 2022
ISBN 978-1-941489-92-5

www.RobertARussell.Org

Table of Contents

Introduction

This book is only so much paper, cardboard, and ink until you make it a guide to freedom, power, peace, and happiness by your understanding and by your use of the principles in it. It will accomplish its purpose and come alive in you only as you embody in your consciousness the eternal truths that it contains and as you put them to work.

If you read the book just for the sake of entertainment, you will be disappointed. But if you read it for the purpose of eliminating fear and worry from your life, you will become free from them. You will find the courage and faith that you seek.

What are the rules and principles essential to the mastery of fear and worry?

I. THE FIRST ONE IS RESOLUTION.

You must not only read with the hope of finding an escape from the restrictive influence of fear and worry, but you must also have an all-consuming determination to learn the way out of your dilemma. This book contains everything necessary for your release from the thralldom of fear and worry. Determine that you will make this freedom yours. Make your study the paramount thing in your life while you are making your demonstration. Say each day as you take up your study:

I KNOW THAT THE ACTIVITY OF THESE IDEAS
PENETRATES ANY DOUBT OR APPREHENSION
IN MY MIND, CASTS OUT MY FEAR, REMOVES

MY UNCERTAINTIES, CLEARS AWAY ALL
HINDRANCES, AND PERMITS THAT WHICH
IS STRONG, COURAGEOUS, AND TRUE TO BE
REALIZED. I HAVE ABSOLUTE FAITH THAT THE
SUGGESTIONS I ACCEPT WILL BE MANIFESTED
IN MY LIFE. TURNING MY FEARS INTO FAITH
AND MY BONDAGE INTO FREEDOM.

II. THE SECOND REQUIREMENT
IS ASSIMILATION.

You should never leave a statement or suggestion in the book
until you have thoroughly digested and assimilated it. You
must synthesize the corrective and positive suggestions with
the creative powers of your subconscious mind. Fear is an
emotion; to over it, you must introduce a new idea that is
stronger than the idea which caused the fear and the resultant
worry. The change is a matter of displacement and substitution.
The antidote of fear and worry is faith. When faith comes in,
fear and worry go out. You probably have your own method
f studying a metaphysical book. If you haven't, let me suggest
that you first read the book as a whole, and then read it again
slowly and thoughtfully, stopping frequently to contemplate
the suggestions and to figure out just where and how you can
apply each suggestion to your life and needs.

III. THE THIRD REQUIREMENT IS THE
EMBODIMENT OF SUGGESTION.

When you find a statement that strikes you forcibly, underscore
it or write it in your notebook. This activity will help to make
your study and practice more successful by helping to embody

the suggestions in your subconscious mind. It will also help you to get to the vital spots in the book with a minimum of delay. There is no short cut to the elimination of fear and worry. The Truth must become a part of the warp and woof of your consciousness.

IV. THE FOURTH REQUIREMENT IS TRANSLATION INTO ACTION.

"Be ye doers of the word and not hearers only, deceiving your ownselves." Bernard Shaw was right when he said. "If you teach a man anything, he will never learn." What did he mean? Most of us learn by doing. Learning is a matter of using what you hear or read. In other words, the suggestions and instructions in the book must get below your neck. They must be set in action through daily practice and application. They must come alive through recognition and realization. We should remember that we are not primarily trying to raise and expand the intellect through our study; we are attempting to form a new habit — a habit that will keep us free as long as we live.

V. THE FIFTH REQUIREMENT IS DISCIPLINE.

There are many aids that one may employ to keep the mind moving toward its goal; one of the most effective is to set up a Fear-and-Worry-Bank. This can be done by keeping a little locked box or child's bank in a conspicuous place in the home — say on the dining room table or on the mantelpiece — and by putting a dime or a quarter in the box every time you violate any one of the principles in the book. If you do this every time that you feel fearful or worried or express a negative thought, you will soon cure yourself of this bad habit.

The money in the box, of course, should be dedicated to some worthy cause.

VI. THE SIXTH REQUIREMENT IS TO INVENTORY RESULTS.

Inventory periodically the results of your efforts to apply these principles in order to strengthen your defenses. List your improvements and successes as well as your mistakes and failures. Determine to make a good record better and a bad one good. Profit by your mistakes. Rejoice in your victories. Keep an accurate record of your experience in applying these truths. List all the interesting and unexpected things that happen to you. This account will make interesting reading in years to come, for it will help you to realize your growth and may inspire you to help others.

Chapter I

THE KEY

"Thanks be to God, which giveth us the victory through our Lord Jesus Christ."

"The Lord is my light and my salvation; whom shall I fear? the Lord is the strength of my life; of whom shall I be afraid?"

"And it shall come to pass that . . . the Lord shall give thee rest . . . from thy fear."

"There is no fear in love; but perfect love casteth out fear; because fear hath torment. He that feareth is not made perfect in love."

"Yea, though I walk through the valley of the shadow of death, I will fear no evil; for thou art with me."

"Fear thou not; for I am with thee; be not dismayed, for I am thy God; I will strengthen thee; yea, I will help thee; yea I will uphold thee with the right hand of my righteousness."

"Let not your heart be troubled, neither let it be afraid."

"Fear not, little flock; for it is your Father's good pleasure to give you the kingdom."

"The thing which I greatly feared is come upon me." By fearing it, I gave it the power to embody itself in my experience.

The Disease I feared is come upon me. By fearing it, I gave it the power to manifest in my body.

1

The Person I feared is come upon me. By fearing him, I gave him power over me.

The Bad Luck I feared is come upon me. By fearing it, I gave it power to operate in my life.

The Failure I feared is come upon me. By fearing it, I gave it power to function in my business.

It is a metaphysical law that everything and everybody in the universe react to your attitude toward them. Your satisfaction, pleasures, joys, triumphs, and victories are self-created. The problems that baffle you, the fears that harass you, the worries that fret you, the persons that annoy you, and the things that upset you act in accordance with the power you give them in your thought. They cannot act in any other way. Both good and evil are states of mind, and both do to you what you permit them to do.

Emerson said, "No man and no institution was ever ridden down or talked down by anything but itself." People may slander and criticize you, but no one can hurt you but yourself. No one can make you afraid, no one can make you unhappy, no one can make you sad but you, yourself. In fact, no one can do anything to you that you do not want him to do. Evil cannot have any place in your life that you do not permit it to have.

It's up to you to determine just what kind of experiences you are going to have in your world. Nobody else can determine that for you. If you are unhappy, it is because, consciously or unconsciously, you want to be unhappy. When you are tired of being unhappy, you have the power to change your consciousness and be happy. If you are fearful, it is because you believe in two powers instead of one. When you are tired of being fearful, you can change your attitude toward God and be fearless.

The ether is filled with negative and evil suggestions that others have used and discarded. But there is no reason for you to take them in and give them a warm bed, good food, and a comfortable home. It is your privilege to declare your spiritual independence, to adopt a lofty indifference, and to shut the door to them. Indifference! What an important word that is! How fraught with power! To the Truth student, it has the same connotation as the word *protection*.

Think what it would mean to isolate yourself mentally from all the evils that interfere with your happiness and peace of mind! Think what it would mean to keep them so far from you that you would never have to handle them! That is exactly the freedom that indifference to evil suggestions will give you. It will not only prevent evil from getting into your life, but it will help to render powerless the evil that already is there.

Fear and all kindred evils cannot live without thought and attention; they cannot operate without co-operation and help.

Evil is neither person, place, nor thing. It has no power until you give it a body or a belief to act with. It comes to you for life, and you give it all the life it has. It holds you in bondage because of the power you give it in your thought. Take away this power by indifference and turn the energy of destructive emotions into constructive channels, and it will cease to operate in your life.

The key to the subject matter in this book is stated in these words: LIFE IS A STATE OF CONSCIOUSNESS. The explanation of all your joys, happinesses, and successes as well as of your irritations, fears, failures, and problems lies in this fact—LIFE IS A STATE OF CONSCIOUSNESS.

Whatever happens to you, whether good or bad, whatever comes to you, whether desirable or undesirable, whatever takes place in your body, in your emotions, in your home, or in your business expresses your consciousness. Experience is the tangible evidence of your collective and habitual state of mind—that is, of your consciousness. The kind of ills you have, the kind of deals you get, the kind of disappointments you meet, the kind of difficulties you face, the kind of people you attract—everything that happens to you is the result of the kind of consciousness you have developed.

You always attract conditions and circumstances that are like your consciousness. If the undesirable and disagreeable were not already potential in your consciousness, there would be nothing to attract them. If you had no mental affinity for them, they would not be attracted to you.

The source of your trouble is never in persons, incidents, or things in the outer world; it is within your consciousness. When you change your consciousness and keep it changed, your experience changes accordingly. If you refuse to accept the suggestion of evil, whether it be sickness, limitation, or trouble, the evil dies or falls by its own weight. Why does it die? Because you refused to support it with the power of your belief. Without belief, it cannot stand. Without your belief, it cannot move. The conditions in your experience are simply prototypes of the beliefs in your consciousness.

The saying, "Like attracts like," means that the effect is always like its cause. If you are a failure in the world, it is because you were first a failure in your consciousness. You were first in mind what you now appear to be. Consciousness and appearance are but two ends of the same thing—cause and effect, *"seedtime and harvest."*

Ultimately, everything in your life comes back to a state of consciousness. Everything stems from that; everything returns to it. Everything is what it is because of your consciousness. Your consciousness is you. It is your life. It is your experience. It is where you are, what you are, and what you have. It will always attract from the world conditions exactly like itself. Would you like to change conditions? Then stop trying to change effects. Stop trying to heal sickness or to improve conditions while your consciousness remains unchanged.

The only successful method of demonstrating Good is to change your consciousness first. It is the first step in every demonstration. It is the fundamental way to change anything in your life. The Universe gives to all men liberally, but It gives according to Principle and not according to human wishes. It does not give you what you ask for or what you think you ought to have. It gives you *what you are.*

The Law says that you must *be* the thing you want. You must have a mental equivalent of the thing you desire. You must have it as a belief. Jesus said, *"What things soever ye desire, when ye pray, believe that ye receive them, and ye shall have them."* The belief is the mental equivalent. When you have that, the answer is just as certain as the light that responds when you turn the electric switch. No force on earth can keep it from you.

There is no such thing as failure to demonstrate. The truth is that everybody is demonstrating his consciousness at all times. Twenty-four hours a day, every day, everyone is demonstrating; that is, he is crystallizing in experience that which he habitually has in his mind.

"Whatsoever we ask, we receive of Him." Many persons think of *asking* as wordy petition to God for a special favor. They seem to feel that God responds to them only when they make some special or unusual demand. That is as far from the truth as anything can be. Jesus said, *"As thou hast believed, so be it done unto you."* It is belief, not words, that brings response.

Your real concern in smoothing out the rough places in your life should be with your thought and not with formulas. God responds to you by corresponding to your thought. The Law of Life says that whatever you identify yourself with, Life will create for you.

Does it require a great stretch of the imagination to see that in reality you have asked for everything you have, whether it be trouble, sickness, fear and poverty, or prosperity, happiness, health, and success? To see that if you hadn't asked either consciously or unconsciously for your present experience you wouldn't have it? Jesus said: *"Every man's word shall be his burden," "Every idle word that men shall speak, they shall give account thereof,"* and *"By thy words shalt thou be justified, and by they words thou shalt be condemned."*

If you do not believe that your present state depends upon your consciousness, take an inventory of your fears, faiths, beliefs, and emotions, and you may be amazed to discover how accurately your outward circumstances match them. Negative conditions did not create themselves; they were fashioned by your thought patterns. They came to you not because you really wanted them, but because you allowed negative images to form in your mind. You were careless in your thinking, and unconsciously you brought negative conditions into your life. But consciously or unconsciously, you alone brought them into being. With God's help, you can and must get rid of them.

But how are you going to get rid of the negative conditions? How are you going to change the character of your conscious and unconscious demonstrations? There is just one way. Withdraw your attention from all that is negative, and substitute positive, constructive thought.

Fear is not overcome by saying, "I am not going to be fearful any more," or "There is nothing to fear." Replace the fear thought with a courage thought by using such statements as these: "I have courage to do what I have to do," "I meet each day with renewed courage," "I draw upon an unfailing Source for courage." In these statements, the undesirable thing is not mentioned. It is ignored. The process is substitution and not interdiction. The metaphysical method is the active cultivation of Good rather than the restriction of evil. When the new image is introduced, the old image fades away.

When you seek to demonstrate the right position or job, you must stop thinking and talking about unemployment. When you seek to demonstrate health, you must stop thinking and talking about sickness.

"Whatsoever things are rue, whatsoever things are honest, whatsoever things are just, whatsoever things are pure, whatsoever things are lovely, whatsoever things are of good report, think on these things," said St. Paul. By steadily and uninterruptedly thinking the thing you want, you automatically *un*think the thing you do

not want. You put the latter out of your consciousness; when it is out of consciousness, it is out of manifestation. Draining the negative of its power by withdrawing your attention and interest makes it futile in your life.

If you want to change conditions, if you want to be more successful, more popular, and more prosperous, if you want better health, greater happiness, more pace, and a greater understanding of God, you must change your thinking to correspond with your desires. Your image of what is desirable and your habitual thinking must "track" together. They must be synchronized. There must be nothing in either to contradict the other. Why? Because it is impossible for the mind to believe and disbelieve at the same time. When the subconscious mind has been given a pattern to work out which the conscious mind does not support, the result is confusion and failure.

To get good results, you must think and believe the same thing at the same time. The new pattern must not only be held firmly in the subconscious mind but must be given the constructive support of the conscious thinking. You must act as though your desire were already fulfilled. Jesus said even before he called Lazarus from the grave, *"Father, I thank thee that thou hast heard me."*

A favorite and much quoted statement of metaphysicians is St. Paul's *"Let this mind be in you which was also in Christ Jesus,"* but they do not tell us what this Mind, or Christ Consciousness, is. They tell us instead of a human mind, a mortal mind, a carnal mind, a personal mind, a fleshly mind; but at the same time, they remind us that there is only One Mind — the Mind of God. It is necessary to clarify this matter, for it is the basis of all metaphysical thinking.

Actually there is but One Mind and but One Consciousness—the Divine Mind and the Christ Consciousness. In the truest sense, there is no human or carnal mind; whatever is designated as such is merely the lack of recognition of the One Mind.

This does not mean that we have the choice of two minds in which to think. It means that we must choose one of two patterns: thinking with God or thinking without God. To be conscious of evil is to be unconscious of God. We have the mind of Christ when we think positively or constructively, when we know only one Presence and one Power in every person, place, and thing. We depart from this Mind when we think negatively and destructively. What we designate as the action of the human or carnal mind is nothing but our failure to use the Mind of Christ, our failure to think with God.

Suppose that you allow yourself to be afraid of someone or something; in other words, you think temporarily with the human mind only. Being conscious of fear, you are, of course, unconscious of God—the Good. You have left His Presence, and you are fearful. What is the remedy? How shall you overcome the fear? How shall you forsake the bondage of the human mind? Become conscious of God's Presence, and you will be freed from the consciousness of fear. This is not a new method in dealing with evil. It is as old as the New Testament itself, *"And lo, the angel of the Lord came upon them* [the shepherds] . . . . *and the angel said unto them, Fear not."*

If you will recall the temptations of Jesus in the Wilderness, you will see that in both instances He overcame evil by substituting the Good. He was alone, hungry, and tired when the tempter (evil the form of suggestion) came and suggested that He use His power to make bread out of stones. It was a

9

negative suggestion, and Jesus reversed it at once by saying, *"Man shall not live by bread alone, but by every word that proceedeth out of the mouth of God."*

The second temptation was even more alluring than the first. Seeing that he had failed utterly in his first attempt, the evil one then promised Jesus the whole world if He would serve him. Instantly Jesus replaced the evil with Good in these words: *"Thou shalt worship the Lord thy God, and Him only shalt thou serve."*

The failure to climb in metaphysical work often results from the difficulty of changing conscious thought. Despite good intentions, some students are unable to change their minds and keep them changed. They do not think deeply or steadfastly enough to change the pattern of the subconscious mind. They try to establish Truth in one part of their mind with affirmations and decrees, and then they deny it by an entirely different set of thoughts in another part of the mind. They need to streamline their thinking and conversation by eliminating everything that denies their goal. If they really want to new image to be acted upon by the Creative Power, they must think harmony with it. The terms, *good, image, pattern* and *mental equivalent* are used interchangeably.

"In all thy ways acknowledge Him." "Delight thyself also in the Lord; and He shall give thee the desires of thine heart." In mental and spiritual work, half-measures never produce whole results. A fifty per cent acknowledgment of Truth will never make us free any more than of a fifty per cent acknowledgment of God's Power will make a visible change in our lives. The Law says: *"Thou shalt love the Lord thy God with all thy heart, and with all thy soul, and with all thy mind. This is the first and great commandment."* Faith must be unconditional. It must be all or

none. If one moment we believe that God is All-Powerful and that He is protecting our loved ones, and the next moment we fear that Mary will get run over, or that Johnny will get the measles, or that we may catch cold, our faith loses its potency.

There are no halfway measures in spiritual work. St. James wrote, *"Let him* [man] *ask in faith, nothing wavering. For he that wavereth is like a wave of the sea driven with the wind and tossed. Let not that man think that he shall receive anything from the Lord."* Anything less than an abiding, irrefutable, and unquestioning conviction about the thing we are doing will bring disappointment and delay. If we waver and divide our thought when bringing forth a new creation, if our assurance is not beyond the reach of uncertainty and doubt, if the attainment of our goal is still qualified by *ifs* and *buts*, we shall fail.

Austin Pardue says, "Treat your mind like the most up to date camera—give them both good care. If you follow instructions, you are bound to have successful pictures. The inner mind's eye gets the best results through concentration. It is even more exact than the latest kodak, with its range-finder, self-timer, and light meter. That which you center your mind upon, that which you focus your attention toward will be marked indelibly within your subconscious self. You will grow in that direction. *'As a man thinketh in his heart, so is he.'* If you constantly hold he best images before the camera, or outer mind, then the finest pictures will result.

"The outer mind is the focusing instrument. It is the part of your thinking that decides upon your conscious action. The other mind, if it is undisciplined, wanders away like a stray dog, picking up garbage and bad companions. The fickleness of the outer mind confuses the singleness of purpose of the inner mind. It starts doing what it is told; then one changes his outer mind, and the inner mind's power is switched over to something else. If one's outer mind concentrates on resentment, hatred, disappointment and fear, one's inner mind will believe that that is the way to look at life. On the other hand, the inner mind is a mysterious entity that seems to do what it is told. It is an impersonal power that does not argue, reason, or debate. Its function is to carry out orders with precision and without complaint. That which you allow your outer mind to think and dwell upon will eventually drop down into the inner mind, and the inner mind will see that it is done."

The victory over fear is not won by arguments or denials or by reading, but it is won by cultivating positive thoughts, by nurturing courage, and by maintaining a firm connection with God. It is much more than fixing your attention on a perfect image of yourself; it involves a determined effort on your part to refuse to allow that image to be destroyed; it is a deep realization that God, the Good, is the only Presence and Power in your life.

It makes no difference what the particular fear or difficulty facing you may be; it makes no difference whether it concerns yourself, your family, your business, or your friends; whether it is conscious or unconscious; whether you are on the battlefield, in a bomber, in a tank, or in a submarine, God is everywhere equally present. He is wherever you are. He is instantly available and instantly responsive. *"Before they call, I will answer; and while they are yet speaking, I will hear."* To know this truth is to be protected against all fear. To practice the Presence of God is to be courageous and strong in every situation. *"If God be for us, who can be against us?"* If we flood our minds with this great truth, we shall effectively turn back every suggestion of evil and every claim of fear.

To change your mind against all evil suggestions and to keep it changed is not only the secret of controlling your life but the secret of great accomplishment.

Robert A. Russell

Chapter II

FEAR — WHAT IT IS

As old Arab story reports a conversation between an Arab chief and Pestilence.

"Why," asked the Arab chief, "must you hasten to Bagdad?"

"To take five thousand lives," Pestilence replied.

Upon the way back from the city of the Caliphs, Pestilence and the caravan met again.

"You deceived me," the chief said angrily. "Instead of five thousand lives, you took fifty thousand."

"Nay," Pestilence replied, "Five thousand and not one more. It was fear that killed the rest."

This is not a pretty story, but it illustrates the ratio of our fears to the evils that befall us. It is as true of depressions and epidemics as of our personal difficulties, misunderstandings, and problems.

The dictionary defines *fear* as "the painful emotion caused by a sense of impending danger or evil." The metaphysician defines *emotion* as "a mental reaction to certain stimuli which may come from without or within the mind." We shall understand both of these definitions better if we think of *fear* as a mental picture, as an attitude of the mind, as an idea that uses us, and of *emotion* as an expression of soul power, or a feeling in motion. If we put the two together, *fear* becomes an intense emotion directed into destructive channels.

Man's worst enemy through the ages has not been famine, pestilence, war, disease, poverty, liquor, organized crime, or death, but fear. It is not only the most paralyzing, destructive, and wasteful of all human emotions, but it does more to build disease, enervate life, destroy health, kill ambition, and dull the faculties of the mind than anything else known to man. Fear is the great nemesis of the human race. It has injured and ruined the lives of more people, destroyed more characters, caused more failures, created more conflicts, and made more cowards than any other cause.

St. John says that *"Fear hath torment."* Fear is an invitation to everything that is undesirable. It works in the dark and secluded places of our minds, undermining and digging into the very foundations of our lives as termites do in the timbers of a home.

One of the classic examples of the power of fear is the story of Job in the Bible. *"The thing which I greatly feared,"* he said, *"is come upon me."* According to the Scriptural record, Job's fear was so great and consuming in its effect that is caused him to lose not only his material possessions but his health and his family as well. It was only when he dropped his fears and changed his thinking that he regained his health and that his possessions grew beyond anything he had known before.

We like to think of Job's experience as out of the ordinary, but actually it is the pattern of every fear held steadfastly in the mind. What crystallized fears function subconsciously) has by the very nature of that mind a tendency to grow. The bad becomes worse, and the good becomes better.

Constant apprehension produces ever-increasing losses, obstructions, and limitations in the body and affairs. If allowed to work unchallenged, fear will keep boring in, keep digging away, and keep agitating until it has undermined and wrecked health and affairs. In fact, there is nothing that escapes the depressing, devastating, and consuming effect of our fear.

"A man's foes," said Jesus, *"shall be they of his own household."* Most everyone carries with him a more or less dominant fear, of which he may not be conscious. In one person the fear may be so strong that it changes his entire character and personality; in another, it may be successfully sublimated that its results are negligible. But uncontrolled fear influences man's life more profoundly than do any of his other emotions. Jesus was right when He said that a man's enemies are the invisible and destructive thoughts of his own mind. Fear is not only an active element in all disease, but it is actively associated with all worry, jealousy, anger, greed, and envy.

There are only two fears present at birth—the fear of falling and the fear of loud noises. We soon begin to develop others, however, and before long we have a terrible array of them. We fear failure in business, failure of health, danger to loved ones; we fear that we may not have enough money to meet our obligations, or that we may lose the money and possessions we have; we fear that we may lose our position, or that another's success may interfere with our own progress. We fear crowds, open spaces, high places, an closed places. We fear harmless animals such as mice, dogs, rats, and cats. We fear the dark, the wind, lightning, and thunder. We fear certain foods or combinations of foods, dust germs, old age, insanity, poverty, heredity, and future punishment. We fear that we may do or say the wrong thing. We fear fire, sex, marriage, childbirth, and journeys. We fear nearly all new undertakings and situations. We are afraid of facing facts, of ridicule, of being unpopular, or of not succeeding in our work. We are afraid that we will do something that people will think queer. We are afraid others will criticize our clothes, our neckties, or the way we do our hair.

In spite of all our vaunted education, civilization, and spiritual advantages, there are still millions of people who are victimized by silly supersitions and the fears that enslaved our ancestors.

It is incredible that otherwise intelligent people still believe that Friday the thirteenth, or walking under a ladder, or a black cat crossing the path brings bad luck; or that two friends looking into a mirror at the same time sever their friendship; or that giving a knife or other sharp instrument to another makes an enemy; or that returning to the house after something forgotten brings disaster; or that owning opals brings bad luck.

What must the Almighty think of those gullible and benighted Christians who patronize astrologers, palmists, and mediums and then worry themselves sick over their dire predictions? Or that vast number of superstitious people who carry wishbones, rabbit feet, or horse-chestnuts in their pocket? Or those others who pick up hairpins and hang them on the first rusty nail they see to forestall misfortune and disaster? When will we learn that nothing of a calamitous nature happens to us except those things that we permit through our own mental attitude? When will we realize that it is the mental acceptance of the thing predicted and not the prediction itself that brings disaster? *"The thing which I greatly feared [had faith in] is come upon me."*

It is not uncommon for superstitious people to defend their superstitions on the basis that they are harmless. But are they harmless? Can a belief that man is at the mercy of the movements of the stars, or of relics, or of signs and symbols be harmless? Can anything be harmless that teaches a man to believe in a power opposed to God? Why do we remain in the grip of the era before Christ when we live in the twentieth century? Why do we follow fakers when we can just as easily follow Jesus? What the superstitious person needs is to have that Mind in him *"which was also in Christ Jesus."* What he needs is the consciousness that knows no power opposed to God. Fear is faith in evil; its antidote is faith in God. The person with great faith in God has no fear.

St. Paul said, *"Put off . . . the old men . . . and put on the new man, which after God is created in righteousness and true holiness."* In other words, recognize the Divine Presence and consciously use It. Bring It into manifestation through your thought and word, not by a direct frontal attack but by the displacement of evil with Good. Let some new purpose come into your life, a purpose so big and fine that it fires your imagination, captures your interest, and leaves no room for fear in your mind.

There are many ways to attack the problem of fear, but probably the best and most scientific way is to study its nature and purpose. It is, first of all, a primal instinct given to man to aid him in avoiding and overcoming the danger.

It is important that we learn early to distinguish between normal and abnormal fear. Normal fear leads to safety and efficiency. The fear that tells us to drive carefully, to get out of a burning building, to run for an air-raid shelter, to look out for trains or speeding motor cars, to look at the label on a medicine bottle before we drink its contents, to go to a doctor when we are seriously ill is a friend.

Abnormal fear, on the other hand, magnifies evil and makes a mountain out of a molehill. It turns the hair white, paralyzes the nervous system, slows down the circulation and poisons the body. It is an enemy. If we accept its suggestions, it will destroy us.

Is it obvious that fear of any kind will always be to us what we are to it? Fear will always follow the rend of our thought. If it is a healthy fear, it will quicken our perception and stimulate us to thought and action. If it is an unhealthy fear, it will paralyze our thinking, ruin our spontaneity, and destroy our self-confidence.

If we are conscious of God as instant and unfailing help, there will be nothing for us to fear in ourselves, in others, or in the world. If we are conscious of God as Omnipresent Life within us, we cannot fear sickness or death. Knowing Him as our Shield and Protector, we cannot fear danger, calamity, or accident. Knowing Him as Supply, we cannot fear shortages, depressions, hard times, or lack in our business or personal lives.

Chapter III

FEAR — HOW IT WORKS

One of the most important means of eradicating fear is knowledge of its operations. When we know how fear operates, we shall be freed from its bondage. When we know how it gets into our lives, shall know how to keep it out and how to cope with it. The trouble with most of us is that we are not generally aware of fear until after it has us in its toils. We know that we are in trouble, but we do not recognize its source.

Fear, like all other negative emotions, operates as suggestion. It works through our thoughts and beliefs. It we refuse to accept the suggestions of evil, if we refuse to believe in evil, it dies. If we accept it, it takes possession of us.

The Oriental has a clever little reminder of this truth in his symbol of the three monkeys. Reading from left to right, they say: "See no evil," Speak no evil," "Hear no evil." The lesson, of course, is obvious. When the Oriental pauses before the door of his temple, removes his sandals and touches his eyes, his ears, and his lips, he believes that evil drops out of his life. He is saying with Habakkuk that God is *of purer eyes than to behold evil, and canst not look on iniquity."*

We like the custom very much, for it is just another way of making us conscious of the need to prevent evil suggestions from getting into the mind. We believe, however, that there should be five monkeys instead of three. To close the door of consciousness tightly, we should add two more monkeys —

"Fear no evil" and "Think no evil." If it is true, as science declares, that mind and not matter sees, hears, feels, and speaks, we must control evil suggestions at their source.

When we have learned to place the seal not only upon our eyes, lips, and ears but upon the mind itself, we shall have entered into that *"peace which passeth all understanding."* We shall have come to that place in consciousness to which Jesus referred when He said, *"The prince of this world cometh, and hath nothing in me."* What did He mean by that statement? He meant that no thought of fear, or trouble, or sickness, or limitation could enter His experience because there was nothing in His consciousness to attract it.

Evil suggestions come rushing and pressing against us, but they cannot press in on the consciousness that is positive to Good, for there is nothing in that consciousness to attract or hold them. When we refuse to give evil eyes to see with, lips to speak with, ears to hear with, emotions to feel with, and minds to think with, evil will drop out of our lives and we will find ourselves happy, whole, prosperous, and well. When evil *"hath nothing"* in us, it plays no part in our lives.

We humans with our fears are very much like monkeys with their traps. To capture monkeys in Africa, hunters use cocoanuts. First, they hollow the cocoanuts out through a small hole in one end, and then they drop in a handful of nuts. The monkey seeing the nuts thrusts in his hand and grabs a fistful. He looks wonderfully pleased until he finds that his fist clenched full of nuts is too big to get back through the hole. Does the monkey let go of the nuts and escape the hunter? Not by a jugful. He screams and chatters, jumps up and down, and rolls over, but he does not let go.

The fearful person gets caught in much the same manner. In a moment of fleeting panic, he becomes afraid. Through some suggestion, he grabs hold of a fear and thrusts it down deep into subconscious mind. It strikes him at his weakest spot and, as is always the case with volatile and explosive thoughts, there is an immediate reaction in his mind and body. He shudders and shakes, but he won't let go. He refuses to face his fear and is caught in its deceitful embrace.

It is a fact that animals will attack a man only when he is afraid of them. Human fear throws out a subtle effluvia which the animal smells, and this in turn arouses a corresponding fear in the animal; consequently, he attacks for self-protection. It doesn't make any difference, you see, whether it be in the animal kingdom or the human kingdom, fear always attracts the worst.

If a man is afraid of life, he will attract the worst from life. He will give the impression of timidity, incompetence, indecision, vacillation, lack of self-confidence; these impressions hurt his chances and cause others to take advantage of him. The fearless man, on the other hand impresses his power, confidence, and self-assurance upon all those with whom he comes in contact.

Now what is the difference between these two men? Just a difference in attitude. The law of attraction is at work in both cases. The first man uses the law destructively, but the second man uses it constructively. The first man uses the law through an attitude of fear; the second man uses it through an attitude of faith.

There is just one law, but there are many ways of using it. It responds to our attitudes and states of mind just as steel filings are attracted to a magnet. If we fear a thing, we attract it to us just as surely as if we asked for it. The mental attitude of fear acts like a magnet in attracting to us the people, things, objects, and circumstances that are in harmony with it.

The reason the things we fear come upon us is that we allow negative images to form in the mind. When we desire or fear a thing, we make a mental picture of the thing that sets the law in motion. Then we think about it, brood over it, and feed it with our thought until finally we draw it to us. St. Paul says, *"Faith is the substance of things hoped for, the evidence of things not seen."* There is but one Substance out of which everything is made. This is the Universal Substance through which the results of our thinking are made tangible. It is so sensitive to our thought that it is moulded by it.

Then why do we not use this power to mould the things we need instead of the things we do not need? Why do we waste it in fear, argument, worry, criticism, anger, and greed, when what we want is courage, peace, confidence, trust, love, and supply? Why do we fill our minds with thoughts of sickness, poverty, bitterness, murder, hate, war, robbery, and ill will, when we want health, wealth, and good will? Why should be not mould the pure Substance of God into the things we really desire?

Fortunately, most of our fears are short-lived. They linger only for a few hours or days, and then they are gone. They are great wasters of energy and substance, to be sure, but we do not live with any one of them long enough to put the law of attraction into operation. A seated fear, on the other hand, is like a two-way magnet. It not only forms and draws the thing we fear toward us, but it also forces us toward the thing itself.

Probably no one can prevent evil suggestions from coming to him any more than he can prevent the birds from flying over his head, but everyone can keep the suggestion of fear from taking root in his life. He can do it by changing the polarity of his faith. He can do it by learning to think what he wants and to stop thinking what he does not want.

The man who is in difficulty or trouble needs to make the most of what he has. He needs a calm and balanced mind and intact faculties. If he is fearful, he incapacitates himself for doing his best, and others sense his spirit of cowardice and defeat and shun him. If he goes about with an attitude of discouragement, fear, and self-distrust, other people feel his negative qualities of mind and govern themselves accordingly.

Would you like to know how to triumph over your fears? Emerson said, "Do the thing and you have the power. They who do not do the thing do not have the power." If you want to put yourself under the law of attraction instead of the law of repulsion, you must change your consciousness. You must watch your thoughts, your mental attitudes, and your words all day long.

Are you negative at the present time? Then start at once to think about God. Put God in the place of every negative thought as it comes along. Fill your mind with thoughts of courage, enthusiasm, self-confidence, and success. Stop judging according to appearances. If things seem particularly bad, keep repeating the words: *"If God be for us, who can be against us?"* Say them over and over again until you believe them. You will be amazed at the lightning-like speed with which circumstances and conditions will change. Instead of going out to seek opportunities, persons, and things, you will find that these will now seek you. They will come to you because of the new images in your mind and because of the Law of Attraction which says, *"Seek ye first the kingdom of God and his righteousness; and all these things shall be added unto you."*

Do you have an important letter to write? Then become still and say, "God, think Thy thoughts in my mind. What dost Thou desire written? Here is my hand; use it. Pour Thy wisdom through my hand."

We have all heard many times that "Thoughts are things," and some of us many have challenged the truth of the statement. The dictionary defines *thought* as an idea or concept, and the metaphysician defines it as a movement of consciousness. Thoughts are things because they have the power to objectify themselves. We know that sick and defective thoughts of God and Truth bring strength and health to the body. We know that inflammatory conditions in the body are greatly aggravated by worry and by concentrating the mind upon them. We know further that it is not the smile on the face that makes a man happy, but happiness in the heart that produces the smile.

If you do not believe that "Thoughts are things," watch the people who have vicious mental attitudes, violent tempers, and explosive passions and compare their lives with those of the persons who have tranquil minds and joyous, uplifting thoughts and emotions, and you will never doubt again. The truth is that every thought is constantly sending a succession of vibrations through the nerves, cells, and muscles of the body and is producing an effect exactly like its cause.

Yes, thoughts are the realest of all real things. When we understand what the negative variety of thought does to us, we shall avoid it as we would the small-pox. Let the angry man breathe into a glass tube, and his breath will leave a brownish deposit on the glass. Scrape this off and give it to a guinea pig, and it will kill it. We do not know, of course, just what mental states cause the various physical ills from which we suffer, but the mental chemist could tell us in detail. It is sufficient to know that discord in the mind produces discord in the body and that, if the mind were always in harmony, the body could never be sick.

Man's mind is like a great mental radio station. It is constantly sending out messages of faith or fear, good or evil, health or sickness, riches or poverty, according to the character of his thought. These messages are flying from us with lightning-like speed in every direction and bringing back circumstances, conditions, people, and things that are identical with the mental attitude or concept that sent them out.

Just as there are air currents in the atmosphere and ocean currents in the seas, there are thought currents in the mental realm. There are thought currents of fear and of faith; there are thought currents of fear and of faith; here are thought currents of prosperity and of depression, thought currents of peace and of discord. Each thought is tuned to a certain wave length according to the intensity of one's belief, and each radiates from the thinker to immeasurable distances.

We shall think of mind, then, as a great magnetic field in which our thought operates; we shall think of our attitudes and concepts as push buttons that right bells in the soul and tune us in to circumstances and conditions like our thought. The same ether that brings us jazz and swing music also brings us the great classics and symphonies, depending upon the button we push. The SUCCESS station puts us in touch with the success currents of the world just as the FAILURE station puts us in touch with the failure currents. But the station we tune in brings us the people, conditions, and things that correspond exactly with the state of mind creating that wave length.

If we persist in living and thinking on the negative side of life, we shall have not only our own destructive thoughts to contend with but the destructive thoughts of the entire world. That is what people mean when they say such things as "It never rains but it pours," "Trouble never comes singly," "I'm in a vicious circle."

If we think and talk defeat we shall be buttressed in our belief by the millions of other defeatist thoughts that are circulating in the ethers. What is worse we shall attract people and events that correspond to our own state of mind.

Most people when they are ill or in trouble want everybody to know it. They believe that misery loves company, and they get a vague sort of satisfaction out of syndicating their miseries and publicizing their ills. When will people learn that it is easier to heal one thought of sickness (their own) than it is the thought of as many people as know about their illness? When will they learn that the fewer people who know about their illnesses and troubles the sooner they will be healed? Jesus said, *"Abide in me."*

The Bible says, *"Cast your bread* [thought] *upon the waters* [ether]; *for thou shalt find it after many days."* Thoughts return to us with increased power. What we send out returns to us with clocklike regularity. Regardless of the thought used, the thinker himself feels the effect of it. If we use a thought loaded with hate or bitterness, it will return in time to explode in our own back yard. If we use a thought of blessing, it will return to bless us.

Our thoughts have the power to make us or to break us. Positive and constructive thoughts are like good food; they give nourishment and strength to the mind and body. Negative and destructive thoughts are like poison; they devitalize the mind and weaken the body. Thoughts may be weights or wings; they can bind us or set us free. They can peg us down or life us up. They can put trouble into our life or take trouble away. Like the push button, every thought "rings the bell" somewhere in the great Universal Mind. Whether friend or enemy responds depends upon the nature of the thought.

It would, of course, be interesting to watch the evolution of a thought from the time of its conception right through to its materialization, but at present we can only imagine what goes on in the mind when we think. As far as we know, the thinking process is very similar to what happens when we throw a stone into the center of a pond. Conscious thinking, we say, takes place in the center of consciousness and moves out from the center to circumference, exerting an effect upon everything within its field of influence. Let us think of our consciousness as a pond, and let us imagine that we have just thrown a stone into its center, the stone, of course, symbolizing the thought or impulse which is being sent out. What happens? There is an immediate release of energy by the impact of the stone (thought) upon the water, and the energy spreads from the point of contact in the form of waves, each wave making an ever-widening circle. Did the water move when we threw the stone into the pond? No, it had the appearance of moving, but the water itself did not move.

All energy travels as waves, expanding in circles from the center where the energy originated. "Light," Dr. Southard says, "consists of waves in ether, while sound consists of waves in the air, but both travel in the same way. The radio waves that are bringing you entertainment at this moment are waves in the ether, traveling with the speed of light from the broadcasting station. Wherever waves of energy are found there is somewhere a center of activity from which they radiate. It may be a powerful radio station, the sun, or a pebble striking the water."

Our chief concern at the moment is not with light waves, heat waves, or sound waves, but with mental waves. There is evidence now that man's mind is constantly sending out through his thought waves of energy that initiate certain activities and cause definite results.

Thoughts are things. Thoughts are creative. They work in accordance with their nature. If you do not like the results of your thinking, do not blame the thought but blame your choice of thought. When you choose better thoughts, they will do better work. When you send out thoughts that are in accordance with your desires, they will accomplish the things you want done. But whether you get what you want or what you do not want, it is always your thought that determines the results. Thoughts make the crooked places straight or make straight roads crooked; they spoil your plans or carry them out.

If your thought is negative when you have an important job to do, it will produce discord, chaos, and failure. If it is positive, your thought will produce harmony, order, and success. But it is always your thought about the work that supports you and not the actual work that you do. There is a vast difference, you see, between being the servant of a thought and having a thought for a servant. Since you choose your thoughts and give them life through your consciousness, you also have the privilege of choosing the ones fitted to do the work you want done.

But stop a moment and consider the thoughts you are thinking right now. What kind of thoughts were you thinking before you picked up this book? Are they the kind of thoughts that re going to prepare the way for the things you want done, or are they going to hinder you? Has it occurred to you that the thoughts you are thinking right now may be preparing success or failure, health or sickness for you in weeks, months, or years ahead? Has it occurred to you that the thoughts you are sending out today will have a tremendous influence on the circumstances and conditions you will meet tomorrow?

Let us suppose that you have a weighty problem to be solved. If you are afraid of your ability to solve it, if you are worrying about it, you are sending forth fear thoughts to mess it up. You are complicating what otherwise might have been a very simple matter. By doubting your own ability to solve the problem, you are obscuring the solution.

The practical way to solve a problem of any kind is first, to turn away from it, remembering Jesus' command, *"Get thee behind me"*; second, to send forth thoughts of faith, self assurance, and self confidence. You must know that you are God-controlled and that your thoughts of faith and confidence have right of way over everything else. You must know that nothing can prevent their accomplishing what you send them out to do.

If I charge my word (thought) with interest and power as I would charge an electric battery with electricity, *"it shall not return unto me void, but it shall accomplish that whereto I sent it."*

What is the most important thing in overcoming discord or trouble? What is the determining factor in success or failure? There can be but one answer — the mental preparation, the change in consciousness. It is just as though you had been trying for a long time to do something alone and, after many failures, had decided to call for help. What does the Father say when you call upon Him? Just this "Step aside," "Get out of the way." Jesus showed that He understood this perfectly; He said, *"I must be about my Father's business."* He meant that God was working through His consciousness and that He must not erect obstacles to His good by negative or double-minded thinking. He knew that He should be an open channel through which the Divine Power could operate.

If you have a pencil near at hand, underscore that last sentence and remember that it applies to you. Remember that you are a center of divine activity just as Jesus was and that God can do for you only what He can do through you. *"In such an hour as ye think not, the Son of Man cometh."* Remember also that He can do nothing for you until you have synchronized your thought with your desire.

The Father's business is always the best that you can conceive for yourself or for others. It is always beneficial, constructive, and upbuilding. If you are sending out thoughts of this character, you are *"about the Father's business"* and are attracting Good into your life; but if you are sending out destructive thoughts, you are a center of destructive energy. You are about the devil's business instead of the Father's, and the devil (divided mind) always brings the worst instead of the best.

"Choose you this day whom ye will serve" —God or mammon, fear or faith. If you go out on the icy pavements fearing you may fall your fear increases your danger of falling many times. If you fear the outcome of any undertaking or business deal, your fear increases the possibilities of failing. If you fear an accident on the highway in your car, your fear prepares

the place for the accident long before you reach the spot. But if you have confidence in the thing you want to do and know that God is doing it and not you, you will travel every road, meet every emergency, and face every problem with speed, safety, and success.

If you are in a bottle-neck and do not know just what to do or which way to go, say with deep conviction:

INFINITE WISDOM NOW REVEALS TO ME THE WAY I SHOULD GO.

If your way seems blocked and hazardous, then send this thought:

THE SPIRIT OF THE LORD GOES BEFORE ME AND MAKES EASY AND SUCCESSFUL MY WAY.

Always put the problem in God's hands first, knowing that it will be taken care of. Let go of it. Change your thought from personality (problem) to God and rejoice that the problem is being solved. See His power radiating from you in great waves of constructive energy, destroying everything that is evil in your life and establishing only those things which are good.

"And Moses said unto the people, Fear ye not, stand still, and see the salvation of the Lord, which He will show to you to day." If you have ever tried to stand still in the face of danger, you know what a difficult thing it is to do. The children of Israel were on the run, fleeing from the wrath of Pharaoh, when suddenly Moses told them to stop running and to *"stand still"* It is hard to imagine any more inappropriate time to have told the children of Israel to *"stand still."*

When to material sense there is no way out, when every way seems closed except up, there is just one thing to do and that is to *"stand still"* and fix the vision steadfastly upon God. *"Stand still, and see."* There is real vision in that command, for it means that fear will be conquered by the complete realization of God's Presence and Power in the present moment.

When the human mind sees no way through or around some difficulty, *"Be still and know,"* *"Stand still and see."* Change your consciousness from self to God, and a way to escape will be provided, a door will be opened, and the problem will be solved.

One of the real secrets in overcoming fear is the ability to live in the present and to have no thought about any other time or condition. It is a tragedy that old people tend to live in the past and that young people tend to live in the future; both miss the happiness and power of living the present.

Now ask yourself if there as ever been a serious problem or an unpleasant situation in your life that you have not survived. Of course, there hasn't or you wouldn't be here to tell it. Then why not accept the experience of the past as a guarantee for the future?

Why not accept the fact that, since God is always present and is always giving His best, there will never be any need that will not be met. What does the Bible say? *"Sufficient unto the day is the evil thereof."*

It is not the problems, losses, and reverses of today that tear you down, but those you fear may come at some future time. Everyone is able to meet the problems of today; but when he piles on the problems of tomorrow, next week, or next month, he is literally breaking his own mental neck.

One of the most important things in controlling fear is to control the imagination — to refuse to let it visualize anything unpleasant or negative in the future. God gives us strength for each day's work, but if we dissipate that strength in combatting imaginary troubles, we go down in defeat. The wise man does not waste his power on the imaginary troubles of the future; he uses today's energy for today's needs. He so fortifies himself by living in the present that, when disappointments, reverses, and losses come to him, he can say with St. Paul, *"None of these things move me."*

Now we come to the most important factor in controlling fear, the ability to keep the mind on God and off self. Jesus stressed this point in the Sermon on the Mount when he said, *"The light of the body is the eye; if therefore thine eye be single, thy whole body shall be full of light. But if thine eye be evil* [divided], *thy whole body shall be full of darkness."* He is speaking, of course, of the imaging faculty of the mind. In the conscious mind, we have the power to select or reject thoughts. But the subconscious or creative mind accepts and acts upon the ideas we give it. It has no power of choice. If the conscious mind chooses only good thoughts, the whole man will be full of light. If that mind selects fear, superstition, gloom, despair, and anxiety to dwell upon, the whole man will be full of darkness.

The imperative thing in getting fear and other evil forces out of our lives is to change the subconscious thought patterns. We do that in the way that the chemist destroys the corrosive power of an acid; that is, by substituting its opposite, an alkali. St. Paul said, *"Be not overcome of evil, but overcome evil with Good."* In other words, neutralize the fear thought by substituting its natural antidote, the courage thought. If you are filled with fear, reverse the fear pattern by filling yourself with faith. Faith always overcomes fear, just as alkali overcomes an acid.

It is a lamentable thing that so many people go through life burdened with fear when the only thing needed to free them from this bogey is a simple change of thought. The reason fear seems so hard to overcome is that we do so little about it. We continue to see the thing we fear through the human mind, *"through the glass darkly,"* and it always appears larger and more formidable that it is really is. It frightens us because we allow it to remain vague and shadowy. The time to meet fear is now, and the way to meet it is to bring it out into the light. When we change our thought about it, it will disappear before our eyes.

Did you ever analyze your fear? Well, do so right now. Ask yourself what fear is and whence comes its power to paralyze you, to strangle you, and to make you weak. Manifestly fear is a mental picture, an attitude of the mind; it has absolutely no reality or power except that which you give it in your thought. Fear is the neither person, place, nor thing. We cannot see it, touch it, taste it, nor smell it. It is purely a figment of the imagination; the moment we realize this, that moment does it cease to have power over us.

The great defense against fear is stated in St. John's words, *"Greater is He that is in you, than he that is in the world."* To know this truth, to realize that nothing in the outer has any power to harm us except through our thought is to be free from fear.

Would you be mightier than the circumstances in your life? Then start right now to apply the alkalis to the acids. Take each negative thought operating in your life and neutralize it by substituting its opposite. If you feel fearful today, destroy the pattern of fear by affirming faith. Keep affirming it until the positive thought reaction takes its place. Hold the new image until it forms in you a consciousness of itself. Clear your thought of everything that obstructs your belief in the power and goodness of God.

The writer of Proverbs says, *"Keep thy heart* [subconscious mind] *with all diligence; for out of it are the issues of life."* Out of it, God answers your prayers and supplies your needs; out of it, good or ill comes, according to the images in your mind. Keep it tuned to the best and the best will come back to you. *"But if thine eye be evil* [full of doubt, fear, worry and anxiety], *the whole body shall be full of darkness."* It will be full of darkness because you have pushed dark thoughts down into the subconscious mind. And out of the heart (subconscious mind) *"are the issues of life."*

Since all fears rests upon some uncertainty concerning the personal self, the most fearless man is the one who is most selfless, Jesus said, *"Deny thyself,"* and St. Paul said, *"Put off the old man and put on the new man, which is Christ."* These are hard sayings; and like Nicodemus, many of us will not obey. We want to be saved *in* our sins and not *from* them. We are willing to change everybody else, but we are not willing to change ourselves. We are perfectly willing to have two selves instead of one. We are perfectly willing to have two minds instead of One.

Now listen to the Scriptures again: *"Except ye be converted . . . ye shall in no wise enter the Kingdom."* We hear much in the church these days about conversion, but very few really understand what it means. To be truly converted means to change allegiance, or to change identity. It means not only a change of mind but a change of self. It is not acquiring a new consciousness, but changing the one we have. It is shifting the center of gravity from the human to the divine in a determined effort to get the lower man co-operating with the Higher Man. When you are really converted, you simply ally yourself with the Truth of your being and make it dominant; you choose the right and boldly declare yourself on that side. You think on that side, live on that side, and work on that side. *"If ye know these things,"* said Jesus, *"happy are ye if ye do them."*

But maybe you do not know how to *"put off the old man."* Maybe you do not know how to deny the self. Then listen to Jesus again, *"Leave all and follow me."* Leave all the preconceived ideas, opinions, habits of thought, and personal reactions to whatever may be happening in your world. Leave all sense of personal responsibility, care, and anxiety. Give up your tendency to worry, fret, and strain. Surrender your doubts, quandaries, problems, haste, and pressures. Leave all your hardships, disappointments, perplexities, and uncertainties. Let go of your personal prejudices and antagonisms. Give up all feelings of defeat, failure, futility, frustration, and despair. Surrender your negative emotions, your grudges, and your grievances. Stop thinking about your body, your symptoms, your weaknesses, your disabilities, and your pain.

Stop thinking about what is wrong with you and what is going wrong with the world, and start thinking about God. Put Him in all the vacant places of your life. Forget all the bitter resentments, jealousies, and hatreds of the lower man; drop all destructive criticism, cynicism, and skepticism. When you have put off everything that is inimical to God, you will have put on the Christ.

Did you ever wonder why it is that one day you are on top of your world, cheery, optimistic, and happy, pleased with everybody and everything, and the next day, with no change whatever in your outer circumstances, you are down in the dumps, pessimistic, worried, fearful, and filled with strange forebodings? The answer lies in the fact that the lower man is not keeping up with the Higher Man.

There are two ways of looking at life because there are two selves in every man. There is the human (personal) self that judges according to appearances and the standards of the world. There is the Christ (spiritual) self that judges according to the principles of Truth and the standards of God. One sees the dark side of things; the other sees the bright side. One is pessimistic; the other optimistic. One hears the voice of evil; the other hears the voice of God. One makes the worst of life; the other makes the best of life. One attracts poverty; the other attracts prosperity.

We must harmonize these two selves before we can manifest our perfect estate on earth. Harmony can be achieved only by keeping the higher self in the saddle at all times. We must practice the Presence of God in every thought, word, and deed; and we must throw the whole weight of the mind on the higher forces of our being. We must never let the lower self raise his head for a second.

Since life, people, circumstances, and conditions will always be to you what you are to them, keeping the higher self uppermost insures harmony outside as well as within.

Your sense of pessimism will always be in proportion to your sense of inharmony. The world will always be to you what you are to it. It will always react to you according to your attitude toward it. The antidote for pessimism was given to us by St. Paul: *"Be ye transformed by the renewing of your mind."* In other words, put your mind in order, and order will prevail in your world. Your world will right itself. But let your thoughts run wild, let your imagination conjure fear, let the lower man have right of way, and the world will seem dark and topsy-turvy. *"In the world* [lower man]," said Jesus, *"ye shall have tribulation, But be of good cheer; I have overcome the world."*

Would you like to overcome your world as Jesus did? Then identify yourself with God. Form new images of yourself; stay your mind upon them. Think about them, and pray about them; very soon you will begin to live them. *"Thou wilt keep him in perfect peace, whose mind is stayed on Thee."*

Chapter IV

FEAR—WHAT IT DOES

Maurice Duhamel gives us a vivid picture of a man in the grip of a great fear: "The heart pounds like a trip hammer. The eyes and mouth open wide. The skin sweats. The muscles shiver. The hair ends rise like the hackles on a dog. The breathing becomes hurried. Salivation ceases. The mouth goes dry. The voice becomes husky. The throat gasps. The lips tremble. The limbs shake. The eye balls protude. The pupils dilate. The hands clasp and unclasp. Muscular coordination ceases. Intestinal muscles relax. The heart slows down. Surface blood coloration fades.

"The chief reason that fear does all of these things is that it causes us to expand our nervous energies much faster than does normal living; so much faster that our condition in severe fright might be compared with that of a ship struck upon a coral reef and taking water faster than it can be pumped out."

Fear is like steam pressure in a boiler. To be safe, the boiler must have a safety valve or other outlet. If the safety valve is turned off when the steam pressure is up and there is no way for it to get out normally, the steam will burst the boiler. The steam must get out somewhere, and so must fear. If we push fear down into the subconscious mind by repression or forgetfulness, it will cause all manner of nervous disorders and trouble. It will blow us into such a state of confusion, indecision, and helplessness that we are incapacitated to meet even the little problems that come along. It may blow us into such queer obsessions that even our friends will avoid us.

A repressed fear is like a boil. If the poison is let out, the boil will heal and pass away. If the poison is not let out, the boil will become worse and cause other disorders. We are not injured by pressure from without but by force from within. If by trying to forget our fears, we push them down into the subconscious mind, they will cause us to become weak, cowardly, and vacillating. They will reach out in every direction until they affect adversely everything in our lives. Job said, *"The thing which I greatly feared is come upon me."* Some people nurse a fear so long that it gets out of control. They exercise it with their faith and feed it with their attention until it gets so big and so strong that they are no longer able to cope with it. They are then compelled to see a doctor, psychiatrist, or a minister to help them let go.

It would, of course, be impossible to estimate the damage to the human body and to affairs caused by fear, but we know that fear opens the entire system to any adverse condition that may be lurking about.

Christian D. Larson says, "It [fear] changes the secretions of the body, slows down the circulation by a depressing effect on the nerves, produces modified effects which lay the foundation for all kinds of diseases and ailments, weakens the tissue structure so that bacteria can multiply and produce more serious results, and poisons the whole system.

"In fact, in the attitude of fear we absolutely give in to every thing that in any way may tend to get a foothold in mind or body. To live in fear, therefore, is to place yourself in an utterly helpless condition. Among all the undesirable states of mind, fear has the greatest power, the reason being that it is so deeply felt, and what we feel deeply we impress upon the subconscious. Fear can be entirely removed, however, by directing the subconscious to have faith—perfect faith, in all things and at all times."

Nothing can save a man from his fears but himself. To the orthodox mind this statement will sound like heresy, but a moment's reflection will show that it is exactly what Jesus meant when He said, *"Work out your own salvation."* "But," you say, "I thought Jesus had saved us already." Quite true, but only in the sense that He has shown us the way. Until we have appropriated His plan and made it our own, it is still in the blue-print stage. The temple of the living God must be built within. The human self must be crucified and offered up as a sacrifice to God. Salvation must be worked out individually by following Jesus in the regeneration. We must take the steps He took, make the sacrifices He made, and discipline the mind in the way he did.

Yes, each man must save himself, not by the mental and physical ordeals that Jesus went through, but by getting the lower self (personality) and the Higher Self (Christ) together. We save ourselves spiritually in the same way that a man becomes a chemist, a mathematician, or a lawyer—that is, by embodying the principles of our profession. We go to school to become proficient in the arts; we go to church to become proficient in living.

Salvation is full, free, and for all, but let us make no mistake about its natures. God gives us only those things which we embody. Salvation is not a gift until it is accepted. When Jesus said, *"Work out your own salvation,"* it was as if He had said, "I have worked out my salvation. I have saved myself. Now you go and save yourself—not by resting upon my laurels, but by harmonizing your divided selves until they become one."

Do you remember the question He asked those who were seeking salvation? *"Are ye able to drink of the cup that I shall drink of?* [Are you able to let go of personality? Are you able to eliminate negative thoughts? Are you able to nurture spiritual objectives? Are you able to discipline yourself as I have disciplined myself?]"

To most people, salvation is a very indefinite thing. They think of it more as an outward act than as an inward revelation, more as a wordy profession than as a transformed mind. *"I, if I be lifted up,"* said Jesus, *"will draw all men unto me."* Salvation is won not so much by professions and beseechments as by removing the obstructions and impediments so that the Christ can come forth. The Christ is already there. We need only to become aware of His Presence.

The statement, "Nothing can save a man from his fears but himself," does not mean that we do not need God's help in this great adventure. The truth is that we need His help more than ever, but God, being Spirit, does not help us by taking us bodily from one place which we call sin and by setting us down in another place which we call salvation. God helps us in the only way He can, by working through us and fortifying our positive and Christlike states of mind. St. Paul said, *"Let this mind be in you which was also in Christ Jesus."* The only way we shall ever get the lower and Higher selves together is by denying the one (refusing to give it power) and by affirming the other (magnifying the good). Before the Christ can take hold, the personal man must let go. He must be willing to be nothing of himself.

Much has been written in recent years on metaphysical subjects, but underlying all schools of though is the one objective—to bring man back to his Source and enable him to recognize and use the powers that naturally belong to his Higher Self. There are many different approaches to the fundamental problem of harmonizing our divided selves.

In most people, those two selves are at a variance with each other. They pull in opposite directions, setting up a battlefield in consciousness and a strain in the body. St. Paul spoke of this ceaseless conflict as the warring of his members—a contest between two forces for the possession of one body. *"If then I do that which I would not, . . . it is no more I that do it, but sin that dwelleth in me . . . For I delight in the law of God, . . . but I see another law in my members, warring against the law of my mind."*

The human self, the lower self, is composed of personality, human mind, and emotions. It is of the earth, earthly; when separated from the Higher (the Christ Self), it is subject to all the fears, ills, problems and worries that flesh is heir to. It believes in two powers, Good and evil, and it believes more in the power of evil that in the power of Good. Does that mean then that the lower self is bad? Certainly not! The human self is fundamentally good. It only seems bad when it tries to think and live separated from its other part.

"For as many as are led by the spirit of God, they are the sons of God . . . And if children, then heirs; heirs of God, and joint heirs with Christ." The lower self, you see, was made to be dominated by the Christ; when it tries to live an independent existence, it gets into all sorts of trouble. Being conditioned by human and negative thinking and by every form of belief in bondage, lack, and fear, it reacts in a limited and restricted manner. Away from the Christ, it uses its power destructively instead of constructively. Salvation is the process of making ourselves over into the likeness of God. St. Paul said, *"Glorify God in your body."*

The Christ Self is the principle of perfection at the center of man's being; it is the connecting link between man and God. The Christ Self is the Real Self of every man. It is that Power within us which needs only to be recognized and liberated to break our self-imposed bondage and set us free. *"As many as received Him, to them gave He power to become the sons of God."* The Christ Self is a very real being, with the God-like attributes of love, courage, joy, truth, power, and peace. We call these attributes forth and embody them through contemplation, prayer, and meditation, and through the Sacraments. They respond to us by direct impartation of the Holy Spirit.

We all want poised, integrated, and power-filled lives. The way to get them was stated by St. Paul: *"That Christ may dwell in your hearts* [subconscious minds] *by faith; . . . that ye might be filled with all the fullness of God."* Do you realize what these words mean? They mean that the human self (personality and human mind) and the Christ Self (Spirit and Divine Mind) must be harmonized until they become one. This unity is achieved by denial of the self, by refusal to think negatively on any subject. The method is to think constructively about everything and to think it so steadily that there is no room in the mind for fear or evil.

They mean, too, that the human self must give itself over completely to spiritual objectives. This process is accomplished through affirmation and contemplation. Before we can manifest perfection in our lives, we must have a perfect model before us. We must refuse to see anything but the patter of wholeness.

If it is true, as mental scientists affirm, that negative states of mind work havoc in the body, it must be equally true that positive states produce the opposite results. To build freedom, health, happiness, and abundance, we must concentrate upon and affirm poise, power, peace, love, and beauty. We must keep the pattern of wholeness constantly before us. We must consistently substitute positives for negatives. We must train ourselves to see that which is instead of that which is not.

And, last of all, they mean that the human self must take all its concerns, cares, needs, emotions, and energies and focus them on God by minimizing the evil and by magnifying the good. One of the significant things about Jesus' ministry on earth was His reluctance to talk about disease or the evil conditions He wished to change. He took the positive position and held to it until the work was done. He did not tell God how terrible conditions were but thanked Him for the correction even before it was apparent. His emphatic affirmation of the Good overcame all opposition of evil.

But look for a moment at the human self as it functions without Christ. It magnifies evil instead of good. It syndicates scandal and misfortune; it gives graphic accounts of trouble, operations, sickness, tragedies, and accidents. It whispers and hisses. It fears and worries. It believes the worst. It criticises and condemns. When will we learn that man does not live unto himself alone and that those who indulge in negative conduct not only multiply evil in their own lives but in the lives of their loved ones as well? Yes, among the transgressors are people who go to church and pray an make their communions and who often tell you that God does not answer their prayers. Of course, God does not answer their prayers. How could He when the first requirement of answered prayer is to close the door of one's consciousness to everything that denies His Presence?

In Truth, we are taught to look for perfection instead of imperfection, to extol the good and eschew the evil; to praise and not blame; to bless and not curse; to live each day as though the Christ were guiding and directing us; to have a firm conviction that God is the only Power in our lives; to cultivate joyous expectancy instead of ominous forebodings; to anticipate success rather than failure; to expect the best from others instead of the worst.

St. Paul gave us his idea on right thinking in the words: *"Whatsoever things are true, whatsoever things are honest, whatsoever things are just, whatsoever things are pure, whatsoever things are lovely, whatsoever things are of good report; if there be any virtue, and if there be any praise, think on these things."* St. Paul knew that right images held steadfastly in the mind gradually remake the consciousness and recondition the whole life. *"Think on these things,"* he said. Do not just run them through your mind like water through a pipe, but meditate upon them, contemplate them, magnify them, hold them in the mind until they permeate the whole consciousness.

Affirmations are marvelous things, but we never take out of them more than we put into them. To yield maximum results, they must for the time being be made a part of our lives. They must be repeated over and over until they form in us a consciousness of themselves; we must speak them with a feeling of confidence that the thing asked for actually exists and is ready to take form at the command of our spoken word. To make them creative, we must think them, contemplate them, absorb them, and live them.

Affirmations will do for us what we expect them to do and no more. Of themselves, they are powerless; but when they are firmly held in the mind, their potency is almost beyond human belief. If the affirmation fails, it is because we have permitted doubt, fear, or some other contrary thoughts to tear it down, or because we have spoken the words without thoughts or feeling.

The word *magnify* according to the dictionary means to enlarge. We increase the good in our lives by magnifying it, and we decrease the evil by refusing to recognize it. Concentration is the process of bringing all the energies of the mind to a common center, thereby intensifying them and condensing them into one focal point. When the mind is concentrated, it acts very much like the magnifying glass that intensifies the rays of the sun to such a point that they will burn a hole in anything placed under them.

Lack of concentration accounts for many failures to get better results in spiritual work. Isaiah said, *"Thou wilt keep him in perfect peace whose mind is stayed on thee,"* and Jesus said, *"Continue in my word."* Keep the mind focused until something happens. Master your attention. Control it. Attend to one thing at a time. Stop thinking of one thing while doing another. St. Paul said, *"This one thing I do, forgetting those things which are behind, and reaching forth unto those things which are before, I press on toward the mark."*

If you think of your consciousness as a wax substance and the affirmation or prayer as a die making an impression on the wax, you have the whole picture of the creative process of thought. *"Take with your words,"* says the Scripture, *"and return unto Jehovah."* We take the word (affirmation) that represents the pattern or object of our desire and identify ourselves with it; we push it deep down into the subconscious mind. We do this through concentration, or by *staying the mind* upon it. We think the affirmation and speak so positively, earnestly, and convincingly that the subconscious takes up the idea without any hesitation. It is impressed upon the subconscious mind, and this impression not only constitutes the pattern for the new condition we wish to bring about but also sets the Creative Principle and Law of Attraction into operation. It specializes the Law, so t speak, toward a definite end. Then we enlarge the idea by magnifying it (thinking upon it) and holding it until the Universal Substance moulds it into form.

To many people, an affirmation is simply the mechanical repetition of a Truth statement such as "I am courageous;" "I am powerful;" "I am prosperous,"; but there is more to the process than this. To change the life in a given direction, a person must not only repeat an affirmation but must also create a mental pattern (image) of the thing desired. He must identify himself with the new image and feel that it is true of him. He must see himself as actually possess of the quality or thing he seeks. Jesus said, *"It is done according to your belief.* [You must believe that it is true and act as if it were.]"

"Behold, all they [thoughts] that were incensed against thee shall be ashamed and confounded; they shall be as nothing; . . . and as a thing of nought." Fear, like every other negative, must be treated as a thing of nought. Since faith is the only reality, and since fear is faith in evil, to get rid of fear, you must change its image. You must turn it around, so to speak and let it become faith in good.

But how do you accomplish this transformation? You recognize in the face of your fear that you lack courage. What are you going to do? The first thing is to rouse the desire to become courageous. Instead of dwelling upon the negative aspects of your fear and brooding over it, choose some positive affirmation in direct opposition to it, such "God is my all; I know no fear." Then start to make constant affirmation of Truth. Create a new image of yourself in action which you unfailingly demonstrate the quality of courage. Fix your attention upon this perfect image of yourself day and night; allow nothing to destroy it. See yourself mightier than any circumstance in your life. Think on this image, concentrate on it, meditate on it, and magnify it until it reaches your subconscious mind and becomes reality.

"Fear thou not; for I am with thee; be not dismayed; for I am thy God; I will strengthen thee; yea, I will help thee; yea, I will uphold thee with the right hand of my righteousness." Transfer the image to God by the prayer of thanksgiving:

FATHER, I THANK THEE FOR FULFILLMENT AND MATERIALIZATION OF THIS DESIRE. I ACCEPT THY COURAGE. ALL FEAR IS NOW DISSOLVED FROM MY CONSCIOUSNESS.

You must say this prayer with the same feeling of assurance that you would have in turning over a problem to a friend in whose ability and wisdom you had absolute confidence.

"The Lord is my light and my salvation; whom shall I fear? The Lord is the strength of my life; of whom shall I be afraid?" The desire (new image) is now out of your hands and in God's Hands. The rest of the process is simply one of sustaining the contact with the new image with a feeling of assurance from the time of asking until the time of receiving. The materialization will take place when the new image is consciously shared (integrated) with the subconscious and Divine Mind.

"Fear not, little flock; for it is your Father's good pleasure to give you the Kingdom." Our part is to create the image, and God's part is to develop and print the picture. Our part is conscious and voluntary; God's part is subconscious and automatic. In other words, we furnish the blue print, and God, asking no questions, does the building. St. Paul said, *"I have planted, Apollos watered; but God gave the increase."* God will give whatever we ask for if we are faithful to the image we have created.

If we refuse to let doubt and worry tear down what we have so painstakingly built up, if we keep the focus steady from day to day, never allowing ourselves to be side-tracked or deflected from our main objective, the answer will come. The Scriptural steps in a good demonstration are these: Ask, believe, receive. We ask by making a mental picture. We believe by identifying ourselves with it. We receive by acknowledging that what we desire is already true.

Have you ever wondered why two persons in the same school of thought, with the same method, same intelligence, understanding, and enthusiasm, and with the same affirmation get entirely different results, in that one succeeds and the other fails?

We can best answer this question by using the illustration of the moving-picture projector. That which creates the picture on the screen is not the film in the projector but the light back of it. If the light is not turned on, there will be no picture. Now let the film in the projector represent the thought or image in the mind, and you will see why it is that one person's affirmation produces results while the other's does not. It is not the image or thought that produces results, but the consciousness back of it. The thought is but the film through which the power operates to bring the image into visibility.

There is probably no field in the whole world where there is so much parroting and mouthing of promises, affirmations, and decrees, nor where so many people expect to be heard for their *"much speaking,"* as in the realm of metaphysics. We are so busy telling God what to do and how to do it that He seldom has a chance to do anything but take our orders. We keep Him so busy listening to us for orders that the orders are never filled.

When will we learn that *"The letter killeth, but the spirit giveth life?"* The Psalmist said, *"Be still and know,"* and the centurion said, *"Speak the word only."* Do you hear? *"Speak the word only,"* and *"Be still."* In other words, give your image a chance to mature. Give God a chance to act. Begin to see Him at work in your affairs. Jesus said, *"The Son can do nothing of himself, but what he seeth the Father do. . . . My Father worketh hither to, and I work."*

The important thing in spiritual work is power. If there is no power in our thought, our affirmations cannot produce the desired results.

God-Power is latent in every mind; when it is awakened in our thought, it brings forth whatever we have embodied in our mental picture. The image becomes alive and produces results according to its nature.

Let Truth students ask themselves: Am I thinking living thought, or am I thinking dead thoughts? Are my thoughts power-full or are they power-less? Often the unsuccessful person will find that the reason for his failure is the lack of power in his thought. The one sure sign that our thought is devoid of power is the failure of affirmations to exert a corrective influence on our bodies or affairs.

People who are aware of this God-Power within themselves get tremendous results from their work. Failure should not discourage the unsuccessful, however, for the same God-Power is latent in every mind and can be awakened by any who will make the real effort. When we realize that nothing lasting can be accomplished without this Power, we shall be willing to spend time necessary to awaken it. St. Paul said, *"God is able to do exceeding abundantly above all that we ask or think, according to the power that worketh in us."*

Power is a natural endowment, but in many people it is like a lazy river. Many persons depend upon it up to a certain point, but they do not specialize it. They let it carry them listlessly wherever it will.

There is a very definite procedure for awakening this power, but it is also very simple. First, grasp the fundamental truth that a constructive image held steadfastly in the mind can neutralize a destructive one. If you are not wholly convinced of the truth of this statement, accept it temporarily as a basis for action. Insert the positive statement that embodies your desire in the subconscious mind and concentrate on it. Drive it into the soul by concentration and focalization. Hold it with will and purpose. Magnify it with realization. Know that creative power is flowing through your image. Know that it is flowing in the direction which your thought gives it.

Give depth of feeling to your image. Have a complete faith in its power to recreate itself in your experience. Probe deeper and deeper until every thought you think and every word you speak is a power. Don't think, speak, or listen to anything that contradicts it.

"And they were astonished [amazed] *at His doctrine* [teaching]; *for His word was with power."* There is just one Power. The power that makes us afraid is the power that can make us courageous. The power that makes us sick is the power that can make us well. The power that makes us poor is the power that can make us rich. The one Power made everything that is. It knows no difference between curable and incurable. It knows no difference between large and small. It knows no difference between good and evil. It does not know that a mansion is bigger than a cottage, that a million dollars is more than a penny, or that a cancer is worse than a headache.

Limitation is man-made. It exists only as a result of man's divided thought. When the thought is healed and the Power awakened, the mastery of every ill becomes possible. Remember that the Power knows nothing outside Itself by which to divide Itself. It is not a little power in one person and a lot of power in another. It is All-Power in every person. It is instantly available for every need. It responds to every one by corresponding to his state of thought.

The difference between fear and courage is a difference only in our use of power. Fear shuts off the power, but courage liberates it. Let us come boldly to the Reservoir of Power and lay claim to courage as our own.

In order to make our claim valid and to secure the result we desire, we must—

1. Make a mental image of our lives as they would be if courage displaced the fear in them.

2. Act as though this image were real.

3. Hold the image firmly in place.

4. Keep the thought from wandering or becoming inactive.

5. Keep the vision one-pointed.

6. Call upon the Word of God to bring the image into reality.

7. Know that the Word of God is instant and powerful and that it always works.

8. Put power and deep feeling into everything we think, say, and do.

9. Expect the power to respond.

10. Know that it is responding even while we make our claim to it.

11. Act and feel as though all the power in the universe were delivered to us personally.

12. Let go, trust, and believe.

13. Accept the result with gratitude and thanksgiving.

Chapter V

FEAR—WHAT TO DO WITH IT

In the first chapter, we told you that everything in your life acts and reacts according to the power that you give it in your thought. In the case of fear, we said, "You endow the thing you are afraid of with the only power it has over you," and we explained that if you take away this belief in its power, you remove the cause of your troubles. We emphasized the basic truth that Life is a state of consciousness, for we told you the only way to improve the circumstances and conditions in your life is to change your consciousness.

In the second chapter, we explained what fear is and why it must be overcome. We said that it is not only an active element in all disease but that it is the primary cause of all worry, unhappiness, jealousy, greed, envy, and poverty. We distinguished between normal and abnormal fear.

In the third chapter, we explained how fear operates in attracting the worst from life and how it can be driven out by changing the subconscious thought pattern. We stressed the need for self discipline in developing a new mental attitude, and we presented the first steps in overcoming fear.

In the fourth chapter, we explained what fear does to you and how you can displace it with courage and faith. We tried to prove the importance of harmonizing the two selves and materializing spiritual objectives. We showed the need of focusing the attention of concentrating the mind, and of magnifying the word; we gave the technique of replacing negative images with the positive images and told how to awaken the power in your thought.

In the fifth chapter, we will attempt to show you how to give your fears to God in order that your life will be what it ought to be. We want you to be able to place your problems in God's Hands and to let Him work them out for you.

In the sixth chapter, we will show that worry and fear are twin brothers and that worry, the great disease of our times, wrecks lives and brings millions to early graves. We shall give definite measures for overcoming this devastating force.

When the Psalmist said, *"Commit thy ways unto the Lord; trust also in Him; and He shall bring it to pass,"* he knew that the only way to get rid of trouble and fear was to give them to God. We declare to you positively that when we place our lives and affairs in God's Hands and leave them there, everything works out perfectly. Only the good comes to us, and all our problems are solved in the most harmonious and satisfactory manner. Our fears are neutralized, our bodies healed, our minds harmonized, our goals are reached, our desires realized, and our needs supplied.

"Therefore if any man be in Christ [understands and applies the law as Jesus did] *he is a new creature; old things are passed away; behold all things are become new."*

In this new state, every snarl will untangle; worry and sickness will depart; weakness will disappear; problems will vanish; friction will be eliminated; misunderstandings will be removed. All our affairs will be brought into harmonious adjustment with divine law. In fact, there is nothing too great to expect from God when we place ourselves and our affairs completely under His direction.

There are many methods of transforming our negatives into positives in order to make our world conform to our material and spiritual needs, but the simplest, most direct and effective method is the one stated by Jesus: *"I seek not mine own will, but the will of the Father which sent me."* When we learn, as Jesus did, to surrender our problems to God with such abandon, confidence, and rust that we no longer entertain them in our thought, all sense of personal responsibility will come to an end. We will no longer worry or fear about the outcome of any problem, for we will know that we are guided and directed by a Power that cannot fail.

Does that mean that we mentally drop the problem into God's lap and then walk away in the vague hope that He will solve it for us? Not at all. We need to do more than ever before. Giving the problem to God is only the first step. Thereafter we must leave it in His Hands until it has been solved. We do not create the good we seek; we only remove the impediments standing in its way. Our part is to open ever wider and wider the channels through which it will manifest. It is ever true that "God helps those who help themselves" and that he works with those who work with Him, but His gifts always go to men in action.

Giving a problem to God seems like a very simple thing, but actually it is the most difficult part of spiritual work. For some unknown reason, we like to mull over our problem after we have given it to Him. We like to worry about it and speculate as to how it is going to turn out. We tell ourselves that we have given the problem away, but we will still keep it. We are "Indian givers," so to speak, for when we place the problem in God's Hands and continue to wonder about the outcome, we take it right back again. St. James said, *"Ye ask, and receive not because ye ask amiss."* There is only one effective method: Give the problem to God in its entirety — give both cause and solutions.

A question often asked by students is this: "Why, after I speak the word, or say my prayer, must I continue placing my problem in God's Hands?" The answer is, "Because you are still concerned over it as the result of your lack of trust." Few are either willing or able to place the problem wholly in God's Hands and relinquish all claim to it and all personal concern over it. We do not seem to know how to keep our hands off. We have not yet learned how to let go. Although we may do our preliminary work with the utmost care in giving the problem to God, we tend to turn right around again and take it back in thought.

The real secret in giving a problem to God is to cut the strings, to make sure that we have let the problem go, to hold nothing back, and to expect great good. If it is true, as the metaphysician tells us, that God cannot act on the problem until we have given it to Him in its entirety, the speed with which it is solved will be determined by the absoluteness of our surrender.

One treatment ideally should suffice for any need, but it may take weeks or even months before the treatment is completed in our thought. Not until we have fully transferred our faith to the new image we seek to bring forth do we let go of the binding conditions from which we seek release. The Bible says *"Cast thy burden upon the Lord,"* but as long as the burdens are still in our thought, we may be sure that have not really given them to Him. We must learn how to give to God for keeps. We must keep returning the problem to Him until we have assured feeling that it is out of our hands. It is out of our hands when it is out of our thought; God takes hold when we let go.

"Acquaint now thyself with Him, and be at peace; thereby good shall come unto thee." The thing we tend to forget is that God works according to certain definite principles. If we comply

with the principles, we succeed. If we do not comply, we fail. "Draw near to God, and He will draw near to you." Since God can do for us only what He can do through us, the sooner we stop worrying and thinking about the problem and begin to work harmoniously with Him, the sooner He will work the problem out through us.

"Fear not . . . ; for it is your Father's good pleasure to give you the kingdom." It is the Father's pleasure to give us everything we need, but He gives us only what we are able to take. All good is here now. he only thing that prevents God's gifts from reaching us the moment we sense our need is our lack of co-operation. The way to keep the problem in God's Hands is to watch our thoughts and refuse to think of the problem after we have given it to Him. If we do this, there is never any question about the answer. The demonstration comes.

Regardless of what the particular fear or problem may be, regardless of the number of times the thought of it returns, we must keep steadfastly denying it by thanking God for the solution that we know is already accomplished. Fear will stop asserting itself when there is no longer any room in consciousness for it. "God moves in a mysterious way." We do not need to know how the problem is to be solved. We need only to know that for every problem we perceive there is a solution ready to materialize. *"Give and it shall be given unto you."* When you faithfully let God keep whatever you give Him, He will give back to you in abundant measure.

Fear is the original cause of trouble; without fear there would be no trouble. The real harm comes to one not from the thing feared but from holding the thought of fear. It is the action of fear in the mind that causes the improverished conditions in our lives and affairs.

Metaphysicians agree that fear is a belief in a power opposed to God. It is a mental picture or an idea that we permit to use us. Since this permission must be refused if we wish to eliminate the fear, we need to employ the will as well as the mind in combatting our fears.

The will acts in three ways:

1. It chooses what we will give our attention to.

2. It directs the thoughts that center around whatever we have chosen.

3. It executes the commands of the mind.

The will is that which constitutes our individuality, for it enables us to select what we shall do and what we shall be. The soil in the garden cannot select the kind of seeds that it is to receive. But we can select the kind of suggestions that we accept and the kind of thoughts that we think.

An alert will is a great dynamic force springing from the center of man's being that enables him to determine whether a thought shall be accepted or rejected, whether it shall be given or denied power. It is like a traffic policeman guarding the entrance to our minds; no thoughts are permitted to pass in consciousness without the consent of the will.

Do you realize what that means? It means that nothing of an evil character can touch or hurt you unless you give it entrance to your mind. It means that you have absolute power and authority over your own mental world, that you can control that world and make it what you want it to be by permitting only positive and constructive thoughts to enter your mind.

The reason for the fear and mental conflict in the human family today is the fact that there are so many weak and undisciplined wills. In many people, the will is asleep and fails to protect the mind. Instead of choosing what shall enter the consciousness, they then accept the random suggestions that come along. With the door of the mind wide open and the will asleep, they are exposed to every traitor thought that passes their way. When the will is weak, we are weak all over. When we realize our need, we ask, "What is the remedy? How can we strengthen the will and make it do the things we wish done?" We find the remedy in the constant affirmation:

WITH GOD'S HELP, I CAN AND WILL ACCOMPLISH WHAT I SET OUT TO DO.

When you have something to do, will to do it with everything there is in you. In the common parlance of the day, "Give it all you've got." Never surrender to anything less than the best; never be satisfied with anything short of the best. When a suggestion that you do not wish to entertain comes to you, turn your attention immediately to its opposite and give all the power of your will to the new image. When you think, think with your whole mind. When you act, act with your whole self. Do not depend upon outside or worldly aid. Let God do all things through you. Depend upon yourself by co-operating with the God in you.

"Not my will but Thine be done." If our human will is unwise or perverse in its choice of thought, we can always get help by turning to the Divine Will. The prayer of Jesus, *"Not my will but Thine be done,"* immediately unites God-Power with man-power. When man accepts this new-found strength, he has dominion over all things. God has given us freedom of will; for that reason, He does not interfere with our personal plans or affairs. He waits

for our invitation to help. He comes to our aid only when we ask Him. He turns to us only when we turn to Him.

Given the full co-operation of our minds and wills, He can do anything that we ask of Him. There is no need He cannot meet, no path He cannot straighten, and no wound He cannot heal. *"I can do all things through Christ which strengtheneth me."*

Would you like to work through some of the common every-day fears that assail mankind? Perhaps you will find help for a specific need; perhaps you will find a suggestion that will enable you to work out your pattern. The pattern is simply the nucleus around which the subconscious mind builds a perfect manifestation. First, make the mental picture of what you want; then make a determined, consecrated effort to realize the experience which the picture portrays, *"So is the kingdom of God, as if a man should cast seed into the ground; . . . . and the seed should spring and grow up . . . . first the blade, then the ear, after that the full corn in the ear."*

After the new mental picture or image has been created, it must be held firmly in the mind every day. It must be felt deeply in every fibre of the being and continously affirmed as absolute truth. It must always be expressed in the present — it is true now. *"Now is the accepted time"* said Jesus. *"Now is the day of salvation."* Now is the only time there is. If we do not believe that our good exists for us in the *now,* the subconscious mind will not be ale to act in the present. Believe, therefore, that everything exists *now.* Never expect anything in the future.

I. ARE YOU AFRAID OF CATCHING COLD? THEN GIVE THE FEAR TO GOD.

When you sneeze, do not permit yourself to believe that you are catching cold and do not accept from others the suggestion that you are. Turn away the fear thought of cold by going within to that Power that knows no congestion or infection. Affirm:

GOD IN THE MIDST OF ME IS PERFECT RIGHT ACTION. I CAN'T CATCH COLD BECAUSE I AM SPIRIT, AND SPIRIT IS WHOLE AND PERFECT.

Hold this image firmly and continually in your subconscious mind until every symptom of cold has dried up. No matter what the appearance to the contrary may be, no matter how many times you may sneeze, hold to your new image and affirm it until all trace of cold has disappeared entirely.

When you sneeze, instead of fearing that the cold may already have permeated the mucous membranes of the nose and throat, say firmly with each sneeze:

PRAISE THE LORD; HE IS CASTING OUT ALL NEGATIVE AND CONGESTED IDEAS FROM MY MIND.

Realize that since all negative ideas have been cast out of your consciousness, there is no longer anything in your mind that can catch or hold a cold. Believe this and hold to it until the truth of your statement is made manifest.

If the symptoms seem particularly stubborn and persistent, lie flat on your back and relax your mind and body until all tension lets go. Then keep repeating to yourself the words:

THE EQUALIZING, HARMONIZING, HEALING POWER OF THE HOLY SPRIT IS NOW ESTABLISHED IN ME, AND I AM WHOLE AND WELL. ALL THE FUNCTIONS OF MY BODY ARE

EQUALIZED IN GOD. I ALLOW ONLY GOD TO
HAVE POWER OVER ME.

There are three causes for colds. There is draft outside the
body, confusion in the mind, and the fear of both. The draft
closes the pores of the skin. The confusion wastes vitality
and lowers the resistence, rendering the system helpless in
throwing off waste matter. The fear impresses the picture
of cold so deeply upon the subconscious mind that the
physical conditions of cold are produced in the body. Fear
not only increases the amount of waste matter in the body
but it is so destructive in its action that it causes healthy
tissue to become waste. The net result of these three causes,
all of which are mental in character, is a clogged system
and a cold.

The main object in meeting this kind of fear is to keep the
thought from interfering with the natural functioning of
the body and to convince the subconscious mind that in the
Divine Plan we were not intended to have colds. Instead of
giving the power of our thought to the fear of wet feet, drafts,
and colds we must give it to God's idea of perfect health.
When we do this, cold cannot harm us in any way.

II. ARE YOU AFRAID OF SLEEPLESSNESS? THEN GIVE
THIS FEAR TO GOD.

There probably is no place in the whole world where there are
so many sleepless men and women as in the United States,
and yet insomnia is both controllable and curable. The real
underlying cause for sleeplessness is fear—fear that we can't
sleep—fear of the results of our loss sleep. The Bible does not
have a great deal to say about sleep but it does have much
to say about rest. *"Come unto me . . . and I will give you rest."*

"Come ye apart . . . and rest awhile." The fundamental point every insomniac needs to realize is that the important thing at bed time is not sleep but rest and that one does not have to lose consciousness in order to rest.

What would you say, for instance, of a factory manager who left all the lights on and the motors and machinery running when he went home at night? You must say the same thing of a man who goes to bed and allows the wheels of his mind to continue to turn on the problems and worries of the day. The original cause of sleeplessness is a fixation of attention — keeping a problem in the center of consciousness, reliving an experience, reviewing details of the day's program.

The remedy for insomnia is first, to wipe from our minds all the problems and worries of the day, either by a definite mental act of postponement (thinking about something else), or by a deliberate giving of our problems to God; second, to fully accept the fact that the important thing to consider at bed time is rest and not sleep. The three R's for insomniacs are relaxation, rest, and repose. Out of relaxation comes rest, and out of rest comes repose. When we have the realization that rest is the important thing, we shall go to sleep with great ease.

There are, of course, many methods for inducing calm and restful states of mind. The most direct method is by keeping trouble and anxiety out of the mind by abandoning ourselves completely to the knowledge that *"Underneath are the everlasting arms."*

To give the problem of insomnia to God, first relax your mind and body from head to foot and then drop from your mind every care, every burden, every worrisome thought; then keep repeating to yourself the words:

"UNDERNEATH ARE THE EVERLASTING ARMS." I NOW RELAX. I LET GO OF ALL WORLDLY ATTACHMENTS. I YIELD MYSELF COMPLETELY TO THE CHRIST WITHIN ME. HIS PEACE AND LOVE PERVADE MY WHOLE BEING, AND I REST, REST, REST. *"I WILL BOTH LAY ME DOWN IN PEACE, AND SLEEP; FOR THOU, LORD, ONLY MAKEST ME DWELL IN SAFETY." "BE STILL AND KNOW THAT I AM GOD."*

Hold these thoughts firmly in the mind not only before you retire at night but many times during the day. Your sleep will become as natural as your waking in the morning.

III. ARE YOU AFRAID THAT YOU WILL NOT HAVE SUFFICIENT MONEY FOR YOUR NEEDS? THEN GIVE THIS FEAR TO GOD.

Stop thinking negatively on your problem. Let go of it. Let go of it in the same way that you let go of a name or incident you have tried to recall, knowing that your memory or subconscious mind will send it to you. Let go of the anxiety, fear, and worry concerning your need. Give your problem to God. Dwell on the thought of God's abundance; remember that He is the source of all supply. Think thoughts of abundance, affluence, and plenty so steadily that there is no room for the thought of lack.

Isn't God just as able to care for you during a period of depression as He is in a time of prosperity? Isn't He just as able to provide you with a good position when jobs are scarce as He is when they are plentiful? Does God know anything about man's cycle of good times and hard times?

Let go! Let go! Let go! Give your problem to God. Never again mention lack. Stop telling yourself that you need money and don't know how you are going to get it. When you are working with Principle, does it make any difference how many men are out of work? Not if you have faith and know that your supply comes directly from God.

What does the Bible say on the subject? *"Trust . . . in the living God, who giveth us richly all things to enjoy."* His blessings are all about us waiting for us to let them become manifest in our affairs. He has provided for everything we need, but we must accept His blessings in the spirit of trust and faith. If we fear, if we are apprehensive or doubtful, we block the way. God cannot get through to us. St. John said, *"All things that the Father hath are mind,"* and we too can say this. Then why do we not accept His gifts? Why do we not identify ourselves with a new image of prosperity and bring forth His blessings? We can do this very simply by changing the polarity of our thought. Instead of thinking negatively of our problem and voicing fears regarding it, we can think positive good. The problem of supply can be met by the realization of the Truth in the statement that follows:

I KNOW PROSPERITY IS REAL. IT IS MANIFESTING IN MY AFFAIRS NOW. ONLY THE GOOD IS TRUE; THEREFORE, ONLY GOOD CAN HAPPEN TO ME. MY NEEDS ARE ALREADY MET. ALL THAT I REQUIRE IS MINE

NOW. I AM A CHILD OF GOD. GOD IS TAKING
CARE OF ME NOW.

IV. ARE YOU AFRAID TO MAKE SOME DECISION FOR
FEAR THAT IT WILL BE THE WRONG ONE? THEN GIVE
THIS FEAR TO GOD.

When you have an important decision in mind and are
undecided as to what to do or which way to go, remember
that there is One within you who knows and always has
the right answer. There is One who always can give you the
guidance you need. The command is, *"If any of you lack wisdom,
let him ask of God, that giveth to all men liberally, and upbraideth
not; and it shall be given him."* It isn't going to do any good to
worry and fear lest you make a mistake or choose the wrong
course. It isn't going to do any good to rack your brains and
lie awake nights struggling for the answer. It isn't going to
help to discuss the matter with friends.

The only sure way to get the guidance needed to make a
perfect decision is to give the problem to God. Just place the
matter confidently in His hands through an affirmation such
as this:

GOD KNOWS INSTANTLY WHAT I NEED TO
KNOW AND IS SUPPLYING ME WITH THIS
INFORMATION AND KNOWLEDGE NOW.

Then stop thinking about it. Stop wondering. Stop feeling for
the answer through others. Know that God has taken charge
and that the needed wisdom will spring forth. If the answer
seems long delayed, be patient. In God's own way, the perfect
decision will be made. Through His wisdom, you will be
guided into that which is for your highest good.

V. ARE YOU AFRAID OF SOME PERSON WHO IS TRYING TO HARM YOU? THEN GIVE THAT FEAR TO GOD.

The antidote for enmity and opposition is love. Are you the unfortunate victim of some personal animosity, bitterness, or hatred? Then remember that the offending person reacts to you with the power you give him in your thought and that the more you think of him negatively, the more negative power you give him. Your confusion and unhappiness are not due to anything he says or does, but to your belief in his power to hurt you. Take away that belief, and he loses his power over you. Stop thinking of him, and he ceases to be an evil influence in your life.

Can God heal such a problem? He certainly can—if you get rid of the personal consciousness and substitute the Christ consciousness and substitute the Christ consciousness. Jesus said, *"Agree with thine adversary quickly, whilst thou art in the way with him."* To heal a misunderstanding of any kind it is necessary to break with the personal consciousness to rise above all personal thoughts and actions, to forget the incident and everything that has been said or done, and to give the problem entirely into God's keeping.

Personal injuries, problems, and conflicts are slow to heal because we cling to the wounded memories. If we keep returning in thought to the incident, we destroy the healing process and keep ourselves in a state of separation. We must realize that we are not dealing with persons, incidents, and things, but with our thoughts about persons, incidents, and things.

It doesn't matter what the other person thinks or does. It doesn't matter what he says. The problem so far as you are concerned is not with him but with yourself. You are hurt and afraid, and you must overcome your grief and fear. How will you do it? By right activity in your thought. Jesus said, *"Ye shall know the truth and the truth shall make you free."* Just as the principle of mathematics when rightly applied solves mathematical problems, so does an understanding of God as Principle solve personal problems. This Principle is Love and Truth; to apply it you must give Love and Truth the highest place in your mind. You must give them full and free circulation in your consciousness. There must be a cessation of negative thought and a quickening of positive thought.

"Love your enemies," said Jesus. *"Bless them which persecute you."* The answer will come when you get your personality out of the way. The problem will be solved when you give the Christ Idea unhindered circulation in your mind. The misunderstanding will yield to Divine understanding harmony, love and justice. Meditate upon these truths as you face this problem:

I RECOGNIZE YOU, _____, AS MY BROTHER IN CHRIST. WE ARE TWO CHILDREN OF ONE FATHER. WE WERE CREATED FOR ONE PURPOSE—TO EXPRESS ON THIS MATERIAL PLANE HIS LOVE, HIS WISDOM, HIS POWER, CONSEQUENTLY. THERE CAN BE NO MISUNDERSTANDING BETWEEN US. NO MATTER HOW FAR APART WE SEEM. WE ARE ONE IN REALITY. I FREE YOU, _____, JUST AS I FREE MYSELF, FROM ANY PERSONAL ANIMOSITY, RESENTMENT, OR BELIEF IN HUMAN POWER AS OPPOSED TO DIVINE POWER. I LOOK BENEATH THE SURFACE EVENTS OF THE

PAST AND FIND TRUTH. I LOOK THROUGH
THE MATERIAL MAN AND SEE THE SPIRITUAL
MAN. I ACCEPT PEACE AS AN ATTRIBUTE OF
GOD WHICH WE, AS HIS CHILDREN, SHARE.

Say this statement, or one you develop for yourself, over and
over until you are sure that it is true, until you are convinced
that you mean what you say, and you will be amazed at the
speed with which the personal difficulty will be healed. Say it
every time a picture of the offending person enters your mind
and every time you see him. Hold to it until harmony and
understanding have been restored, until a perfect agreement
has been reached. As it takes two to make a quarrel, the battle
will be half won when you refuse to b negative about the
situation. The other person will fell your positive attitude
toward him, and the situation will be resolved. The change
may come in several ways, any one of which you are now
prepared to accept. Your friend may merely change his
troublesome attitude, he may overtly seek peace with you, or
he, along with the problem, may be eliminated from your life.

VI. ARE YOU FEARFUL FOR THE LIFE OF SOME LOVED ONE? THEN GIVE THIS FEAR TO GOD.

Stop looking at appearances. Stop being depressed. If you are
going to work with God to restore a loved one to health, you
must eliminate every fear and worry and give the whole force
of your mind to His Presence.

Yes, I know the case may look bad. The doctor may say there
is no hope; medicines may have failed. But there is still God
who made the body and who is able to restore and heal it.
It makes no difference how complicated the illness may be
now, how low or how far your loved one may have gone, God

is still able to raise him up. It has been done time and time again, and it will continue to be done for those whose faith is strong and whose vision is high.

Jesus said, *"My Father worketh hitherto, and I work."* Ask yourself just what you are doing to help God in this matter. Remember that He works through your faith and mental attitude. He answers your prayer and your belief. Are you working with the forces of life or with the forces of death? Are you thinking with these adverse conditions seemingly at work or are you thinking with the healing forces of light and strength? Are you giving in to the belief in death or are you throwing the full power of your mind and thought on the side of life?

What you give in to usually wins. It wins because you increase the power of that thing in any given situation. Give in to the forces of death, and the subconscious mind will increase the powers of that force. Give in to the forces of life, and the subconscious mind will increase the power of life.

You must never waver for a moment; you must keep your mental attitude steady and true. You must never compromise. If the forces of life and death are almost equally balanced, as metaphysicians tell us is the case, the outcome of a serious illness may depend almost entirely upon your mental attitude and that of your loved one. If you give your mind to the side of life, you help the life forces to win. If you permit your mind to act with the idea of death, the forces of death are almost certain to win.

Relax mentally and physically. Free your mind of any sense of fear or worry. Recognize that there is but one perfect Life that we all share. It is the Life of God. There is no sickness in the one perfect Life, and there is no death.

Know that your word is a law unto itself. Know that it operates through your loved one as Power and Life.

Know that the one you wish to help is one with this Perfect Life of God. Know that Life is in him and that he is in Life, and that Life responds to him through your word. Then call him by name saying.

THIS WORD IS FOR YOU, _____.
THE RESTORING, SAVING, AND HEALING POWER OF GOD NOW DELIVERS YOU FROM EVERY FORM OF ILLNESS. *"HE THAT RAISED UP CHRIST FROM THE DEAD SHALL ALSO QUICKEN YOUR MORTAL BODY. BY HIS SPIRIT THAT DWELLETH IN YOU."* KNOWING THAT DIVINE LIFE IS THE ONLY REALITY IN YOUR BODY, I PLACE YOU LOVINGLY IN GOD'S HANDS. I REST CALMLY AND SERENELY IN THE CONSCIOUSNESS THAT GOD IS TAKING CARE OF YOU AND HEALING YOU PERFECTLY.

CHRIST CAME THAT YOU *"MIGHT HAVE LIFE AND HAVE IT MORE ABUNDANTLY."*

THERE IS BUT ONE LIFE, THE PERFECT LIFE OF GOD, AND THAT LIFE IS YOUR LIFE NOW. IT IS BIRTHLESS, DEATHLESS, INDESTRUCTIBLE, AND IMPERISHABLE. THE PRESENCE AND POWER OF GOD'S LIFE ARE AT THE CENTER OF YOUR BEING. YOU ARE CONSCIOUS OF THIS LIFE NOW. YOU ENTER INTO IT AND IT ENTERS INTO YOU.

THIS LIFE IS SO STRONG IN YOU THAT IT NORMALIZES EVERY ORGAN AND EVERY

FUNCTION OF YOUR PHYSICAL BEING. YOU ARE FILLED WITH THE PERFECT LIFE OF GOD, AND IT MOVES OUT FROM YOU IN ALL DIRECTIONS, DISSOLVING ALL THOUGHTS OF DISEASE AND DEATH.

THE REJUVENATING POWER OF THIS LIFE IS NOW AT WORK IN EVERY CELL AND FIBER OF YOUR BEING, MAKING YOUR BODY PURE AND RADIANT.

THIS WORD, OPERATING THROUGH YOUR MIND AND BODY, INCREASES THE POWER OF LIFE IN YOU TO SUCH AN EXTENT THAT DEATH CAN GET NO HOLD UPON YOU.

I DECLARE THAT THE SOURCE OF ALL LIFE IS MANIFESTING IN AND THROUGH YOU NOW. IN CHRIST'S NAME, IT IS SO. AMEN.

Then rest calmly and peacefully in the knowledge that your loved one is going to respond to your word. Expect him to respond. KNOW that he will respond and have no anxiety about it.

But what if you are called upon to help in a case in which the sense of human life seems to be very weak, possibly as the result of the weight of years? The individual himself may be praying for death as release from his bondage of pain or affliction.

The all-encompassing prayer for peace is, perhaps, the most pertinent under the conditions. With our human limitations, we cannot say what is best for the person whose hold on life has so lessened. But we can give him to God knowing that —

"God is not the author of confusion but of peace."

"To be spiritually minded is life and peace."

"The dayspring from on high hath visited us to give light to them that sit in darkness and in the shadow of death, to guide our feet into the way of peace."

"Her [wisdom's] ways are ways of pleasantness and all her paths are peace."

We can say with conviction —

I SPEAK TO YOU NOW, _____, KNOWING THAT MY WORD *"SHALL NOT RETURN UNTO ME VOID, BUT IT SHALL ACCOMPLISH THAT WHERETO I SENT IT."* THE CHRIST WHO CAME TO BRING PEACE TO THE WORLD WILL NOT FAIL YOU IN YOUR SEARCH FOR PEACE. HE ALONE KNOWS WHETHER YOUR PEACE IS TO BE ATTAINED THROUGH FREEDOM FROM PAIN AND CONFUSION AND FEAR, OR THROUGH THE RELEASE OF THE PHYSICAL BODY. DIVINE LOVE IS AT THIS MOMENT LEADING YOU TO THAT PERFECT STATE WHICH IS YOURS BY VIRTUE OF YOUR PLACE AS A CHILD OF GOD. I CLAIM FOR YOU *"THE PEACE OF GOD WHICH PASSETH ALL UNDERSTANDING."*

Robert A. Russell

Chapter VI

FEAR — HOW TO MEET IT

In the city of Boston is a Worry Clinic to which go people who have worried themselves sick. Their uncontrolled worry has resulted in a host of afflictions: nervous disorders and mental depression, stiffness of the joints, heart and stomach troubles, glandular disorders, skin diseases, kidney and liver diseases, high blood pressure, paralysis, and diabetes. They go to the Worry Clinic to learn how to master their negative thoughts and emotions and to readjust themselves to life.

The Thought Control Clinic is one of the most unique institutions of its kind anywhere. It has been the means of saving countless persons from the vicious habit of worrying by giving them mastery over themselves.

Worry and fear are twin brothers; wherever we fine one, we find the other. Worry is the great disease of modern times; it cripples the body, wrecks the mind, and brings untold numbers to an early grave. Men and women rush through the years, draining their forces and beating out their lives by worrying; through fear, anxiety, over-ambition; and by physical and mental excesses. The pay-off is stomach ulcers, tremors, nausea, palpitation, high blood pressure, nervous breakdowns, and an array of other ills too numerous to mention.

The body does not break primarily because of the amount of work it does, nor do minds become unbalanced because of the responsibilities they carry. Worry and anxiety overload the circulatory and nervous systems to the point of danger, and man runs to the doctor for pills, to the sanitarium for rest, and to the hot springs for baths. He surrounds himself with electrical devices and other gadgets.

The real solution of the problem of worry and the healing of the corresponding physical symptoms result from controlling and spiritualizing the mind. Faith in evil must be replaced with faith in Good. Faith in evil must be replaced with faith in Good. Old habits of thought must be replaced with new habits. Evil emotions must be replaced with healthy emotions. Negative images must be replaced with others so strongly positive that the negative ones are literally destroyed. *"He that ruleth his spirit is greater than he that taketh a city."*

Christian D. Larson says that worry is "one of the chief causes of old age and those conditions of lessened ability and vitality that come with old age. Worry acts directly upon the nervous system, depressing the nerves and thereby producing not only pain in the nerves, but also every imaginable form of nervousness. In fact, there is no cause that produces so many nervous disorders as worry. Such mental states as gloom, despair, despondency, discouragement and anxiety produce the same results. They are all different forms of worry, however, sometimes mixed with selfishness. Their tendency is to depress not only the mind, but the physical tissues. This depression causes the tissues to dry up, harden, and ossify, and here we have one of the principal causes for the stiffness in the human framework that we mistake for old age."

The worst thing about worry is not the great waste of mental and physical energy, nor the distressing and dangerous diseases which it brings, but the fact that it gives nothing worthwhile in return. If the truth were known, it would be found that nothing good was ever accomplished by worry.

It never solved as problem nor healed a disease; it never developed a job nor improved a bad condition.

The chronic worrier holds up his forward move because he first nervously counts the cost. The man who really accomplishes things does them spontaneously. If he worried about what he was planning to do, he would seldom carry his plans out effectively. The positive and fearless man says, "I can and I will," and suits the action to the word. The fearful man has many excuses—"I can't," "The cards are stacked against me," "What if *this* or *that* should happen," "Nothing ever turns out right for me," "I'm unlucky," "I never do anything right," "Suppose I should lose my job," "Suppose I should lose my health," "Suppose I should have to have an operation."

Many persons use these and kindred statements, but few realize the harmful effects they produce in their lives. On the surface, of course, such expressions seem harmless and unimportant, but they create the patterns of defeat. If these statements are repeated often enough, they crystallize into the conditions the words picture.

There is a science of speech just as there is a science of thinking. It is just as possible to talk ourselves into trouble, sickness, and poverty as it is to think ourselves into them.

The truly scientific thinker never permits himself to think of or speak about anything that he does not wish to experience. Realizing that he will be held accountable for every idle thought and word, he confines his thought and speech to that which will work for his highest good. Knowing that the positive thought and word cause the whole power of the mind to work with him and for him in the realization of his goal, he at all times keeps his speech and thinking constructive.

Would you learn the secret of a towering and successful life? Then keep your thought and speech positive to Truth. Use the power of your mind for what you want. Never allow your power to be used for what you do not want.

In the truest sense, you cannot speak negatively or critically of anybody or anything without getting a negative or unfavorable reaction. What we send out (either by voice or thought) comes back to us with unerring precision. What we find in the outer world, we shall find within ourselves.

A wise man said, "That thou seest, that thou beest." If we find deficiencies in our friends we shall find deficiencies in ourselves. What we dwell upon comes to dwell with us just as certainly as if we had deliberately invited it. Our recognition of evil is an invitation to it to become our own. It behooves us to train ourselves to see the best, expect the best, and to speak of the best in every person, place, and thing.

When we speak of ourselves, let us refuse rigidly to voice detrimental statements, such as these: "I am weak and nervous," "I can't stand this any longer," "I am so sensitive," "I am thoroughly disgusted," "I am getting old," "I am getting tired," "I can't do the work I used to," "These stairs are killing me," "My children are driving me wild," "You know I have to be so careful of my heart," "This has been a terrible day," "I have put in an awful night," "Nothing I eat agrees with me," "I just can't remember anything anymore," "No one understands me."

Those who understand the power of thought and the effect of words know that such statements as these are both false and injurious. *"Whatsoever a man soweth that shall he also reap."* If we sow discord, we shall reap destruction. The penalty is swift and sure. No one can escape it.

Summary

Now I should like to summarize for you some of the rules and techniques for overcoming fear and worry.

1. See worry for what it is.

Worry is a pernicious habit foreign to your nature. Contrary to human belief, worry is unnatural. It was not a part of your emotional equipment at birth, for worry is an acquired habit. You had to learn how to worry just as you had to learn how to walk, read, write, and spell. It is a perverted use of the brain that results in a habit that can and must be broken—a habit that dangerously affects your whole life, health, happiness, freedom, supply, effectiveness, and relationship to others. Worry in any form comes from a destructive action of the mind upon itself. It is a psychic and emotional disturbance. When we peg our worries to definite facts, most of them disappear. The greatest antidote for worry is the knowledge that man-power plus God-Power can accomplish anything that needs to be done.

The things which we worry about are like hot potatoes. They should never be handled when first taken from the oven of disturbed emotion but should be allowed to cool. We should make it a rule to never permit ourselves to worry about anything until at least forty-eight hours after it has happened. Then we shall be able to see the object of our worry in its true light. The further we get from the problem the less power it will have over us.

Accept every problem as an opportunity to prove the Truth you already know. Remind yourself that the solution to the problem came into being simultaneously with the existence of the problem and that you have access to that solution.

Know that "*All things work together for good to them that love God,*" that time will solve every problem, and that Love will meet every need.

2. Realize that worry is a luxury.

Worry is an expensive and extravagant luxury because it exacts such a toll in personality, health, peace, and happiness. A large group of doctors who made an intensive study of the subject found that worry is the greatest single cause of sickness in human beings. Forty per cent of our worries are grouped around the past; fifty per cent around the future; and ten per cent around the present. If a metaphysician had been arranging the "Four Freedoms," he would have put *freedom from fear* before *freedom of speech* and *freedom of worship,* for we cannot have freedom of speech and freedom of worship unless we first have freedom from fear. A wise man once said, "If you wish to fear nothing, consider that everything is to be feared. Then you will suddenly discover the things you could not fear if you wanted to. These are the things which will help you when you need help most."

3. Face the problem.

The first step in overcoming worry is to face frankly the problem that is harassing you. It is only a scarecrow, so walk up to it boldly, pull out the straw, and analyze it.

If the problem you are worrying about at the moment has to do with people, face it by realizing that you cannot change people. No person has more power than you give him in your thought. It is not personalities that you deal with; you deal with your thoughts about personalities. You can change people only by changing your mental attitude and your relationship to them. If you refuse to accept the injury intended for you, if you keep it outside your consciousness and refuse to let it touch you, it will lose its power over you.

4. Insulate your thoughts.

Keep a wide, wide space between your thoughts and your feelings. Great worriers are by nature very emotional people. If they were not emotional, they would not be worriers. The victim of worry should never indulge in antagonism, cynicism, hatred, jealousy, revenge, resentment, brooding, suspicion, or envy, for these feelings are loaded with poison. They create the kind of atmosphere and thinking out of which all worry comes. Study the antidote of Jesus for fear and worry, and you will see that it was very simply a matter of forgetting the wrong thing and remembering the right thing. Jesus found fear everywhere. When Peter, James and John fell on their faces on the Mount of Transfiguration, He said, *"Arise, and be not afraid."* To the terrified passengers on a storm-tossed ship, He said, *"It is I, be not afraid."* At the Last Supper, He said, *"Let not your heart be troubled, neither let it be afraid."* To the grief-stricken family of James, He said, *"Be not afraid, only believe."*

Why do you suppose that Jesus had so much to say about fear? He knew that fear is faith in evil. Take time to realize your basic faith in good. Let Christ fill your minds and hearts with His courage, love, peace, power, and calm assurance. Feel every word of Truth that you speak, and fear will roll off your mind like water off a duck's back.

5. Discipline yourself.

Your worry pattern will be effaced when you have disciplined your consciousness so that it stops working on the plane of fear and works on the plane of faith. No matter what obstructions confront you, know that the Law which you are using never fails. Analyze the negatives in your mind (the affinities for fear and worry) and resolve to cleans and purify your mental household. *"Blessed are the pure in heart* [the subconscious mind], *for they shall see God."* Say to yourself,

> I AM NOW CLEANSING MY MIND OF ALL STRAIN, SICKNESS, TROUBLE, INJUSTICE, JEALOUSY, REVENGE, RESENTMENT, MISTAKES, REGRETS, DISAPPOINTMENTS AND DEFEATS. I KNOW ONLY PEACE, POWER, ORDER, PLENTY, FREEDOM, AND LOVE. GOD IS ADEQUATE FOR MY EVERY NEED. HE IS WITH ME NOW. HIS WISDOM AND POWER ARE MIND TO EMPLOY.

6. Develop a good forgettor.

If we *learn* to worry, we *un-learn* the habit by forgetting. William James, the great psychologist, once said, "The essence of genius is to know what to overlook." In other words, never look back, never dwell upon past mistakes. When your thoughts gets enmeshed in fear or worry tracks, choose something positive, quiet, and uplifting to think about. Start and close your meditation with one of the great Scriptural aids to mental health. There are many of these in the Bible; an outstanding one is St Paul's: *"Forgetting those things which are behind and reaching forth unto those things which are before, I press forward."* Memorize that statement right now and repeat it quietly and slowly many times a day. Practice the Presence of God and know that in the midst of all your disappointments and perplexities He is with you. Be imperturable. Practice the art of relaxation, of letting go. Whatever the pressure or stress, affirm with St. Paul, *"None of these things move me."* Worry disappears from the peaceful mind as snow does under the warm sun.

What did the Psalmist mean when said, *"Let the dead past bury the dead?"* He meant that we were to cut off the past with its regrets, troubles, sickness, loneliness, failures injustices, defeats, frustrations, perplexities, losses, strains, and stresses. St. Paul said the same thing in his *"Forgetting those things which are behind,"* but he added, "press forward." Worry is a diseased thought keep active through memory. The greatest obstacle to spiritual healing is the mental and emotional retention of the evil of the past. That is why a poor memory about unpleasant things is a powerful ally to healing.

It is a wise person who learns early in this life to forget the past and to live in the fullness of joy in the present. Is that lesson hard to learn? Not if you work at it. All worry should be put out of your mental house each night just as you put out the milk bottles to be carried away in the morning; you should so completely eliminate it that it becomes a thing from which all substance has been removed. Yes, I know that you have made mistakes, but if you hadn't made mistakes you would have lived your life in vain. If you learn and grow by your mistakes, that is if you use them, you will become a better person. If you do not use them, you will disintegrate.

7. Do not syndicate your troubles.

Do not discuss your woes with anybody and everybody. If you must share your mental burdens with others, share them only with your minister, doctor, or the immediate members of your family. The widespread discussion of your troubles not only accentuates them and fixes them more deeply in your consciousness, but it also creates a community thought that aggravates the condition which you are trying to overcome. If you share your troubles with ten or fifteen different people, you have ten or fifteen minds to heal instead of one. You have multiplied your worry ten or fifteen times. It is always wise to keep your troubles to yourself. The certain shield against fear and worry is the *Practice of the Presence of God.* In Him, there is no pressure, tension, or stress.

8. Keep busy.

Keep busy in time of adversity or anxiety. If you give in to shock or depression and brood over the thing that has happened to you, your recovery will be slow. The antidote for this tendency is intense action. It doesn't make any difference what you do at a time like this, but difference what you do at a time like this, but you must do something. Keep your worry and your business moving together. Meet your problem on your feet. This is one of the first rules of victory. If you succumb to your anxiety, you are lost. Inactivity results in stagnation. Since your body is about 90 per cent water, you must intensely alive and active. Mental and physical activity stimulates circulation and elimination; inactivity slows these processes down. The Law of Life is the law of perfect balance; balance between wear and tear can be maintained only while you are in motion.

9. Remain steadfast and immovable.

When trouble engulfs you, deepen your convictions and make them serve you. What do you believe about God's power of deliverance? If you believe in it, this is the time to put the power to work. Never think of yourself as being the victim of circumstances. Awaken the sleeping Giant within you ad cooperated with the power of your soul and mind. Be positive, and you will get positive results. Be negative, and you will get negative results. Worry, like all other negative emotions, follows the law of consciousness. Fear and worry patterns have been made by a perverted use of consciousness; they can be unmade by the habitual contemplation of that which is good and desirable. Is that hard for you to understand? Then think of fear and faith as two ends of the same thing. Fear is faith manifesting at a low degree. Change your consciousness, and what happens? You turn your problem upside down (or I should say right side up). Instead of manifesting *fear,* you now manifest *faith.* You hold to the promise, *"He will keep him in perfect peace, whose mind is stayed on Thee."*

Robert A. Russell

Chapter VII

"BE NOT AFRAID"

"Be strong and of good courage; be not afraid neither be thou dismayed; for the Lord thy God is with thee withersoever thou goest."

God has not commanded us to do anything that we cannot do. The courage that we are asked to manifest we already possess, for it is the Spirit of Christ in us. It of itself is mightier than any situation or circumstance. It is ours in the same way that Life, Love, Power, and Mind are ours. If it were not already ours we could do nothing to make it ours. Courage is not something that has to be made, grown, or thought out. It already exists; it awaits only our recognition and use. Courage is the way of deliverance from fear and the way to all achievement. The courageous man is the fearless man.

The strong man is the dauntless man. Be dauntless. Let God convert your fear to faith and your doubt to certainty. Let your courage manifest itself in everything you think, say and do. Examine yourself frequently to make sure that no force of evil, past present, or future is assailing you from the outside. Rest in the realization of your Inner Power. Claim God as your instant and unfailing help.

Accept as true Paul's statement: *"In Him, we live and move and have our being."* Learn to see God in every circumstance, condition, person, place, and thing. Take Him as your companion. *"Acquaint now thyself with Him and be at peace."* Let Him be your partner. Believe in His Presence. *"Lo, I am with you always,"* He has said. Accept your unity with the All-Good. Identify yourself with Him.

Say often—so often that the truth in the words forms your basic attitude toward the world and all the persons, places, and happenings in it—

I HAVE TRUE COURAGE, FOR I AM UNIFIED WITH GOD. I AM ONE WITH LIFE, LOVE, TRUTH, INTELLIGENCE, POWER, PEACE, AND JOY. I AM NOT AFRAID, FOR I TRUST IN HIM.

When you are identified with God, you are identified with His courage, and courage overcomes fear. It is not the object of fear that we need to deal with but fear itself. There is nothing you can fear that is half so bad as the fear of it. Emerson said, "Never set a sail to fear." Do you realize that you can use fear to develop faith and courage? The depth of your valley is the height of your mountain. The depth of your fear is the height of your courage. If fear is faith in evil, reversing the fear results in faith in God. The further down you go in fear, the higher up you can go in faith. Have you touched bottom with your fear? Then you are ready to climb the heights.

Is that hard to understand? Then let us present it in another way. Fear generates destructive energy. In metaphysics, we think of fear as energy in reverse, energy flowing in the wrong direction, energy moving away from good instead of towards it. Just as misdirected electrical energy burns out a light bulb, a vacuum cleaner, or a generator, fear energy slows down all the functions of mind and body. It lowers resistance, weakens efficiency, and cripples ability.

Would you bring God in to your world? Then be still and let your subconscious work. Your subconscious is equal to any and every demand you can make upon it. In order to get your subconscious mind working for you, you have to keep it steady, quiet, purposeful, and peaceful. Here is the place in which the Holy Spirit does his work. *"Be still and know that I am God,"* *"Be still."* Know the truth. Practice the Presence by keeping an unbroken connection with your subconscious mind. Let the sound of the motor of your car, the beat of your heart, the rhythm of your footsteps, the wheels in a nearby factory furnish an accompaniment to the Truth that you seek to embody your life. *"Be still."* *"Be still and know."* *"Be still and know that I am God."*

Emerson said, "Do the thing you are afraid of, and the death of fear is certain." If you are afraid to fly, take a ride in an aeroplane. If you are afraid of people, cultivate their presence. If you are afraid of water, learn to swim. If you are afraid of horses, learn to ride. If you are afraid of closed places, go into them until you have mastered that fear. If you are afraid of dogs, study them and take an interest in them. "The best remedy for cold feet," someone said, "is to stand on them." It doesn't make any difference what you dread to do, you will find that you have the power to carry it through when you embark upon the necessary action.

There is a Spirit in you that is strong, courageous, fearless, and free. To be aware of this Spirit makes you greater than any situation or circumstance. This knowledge in itself is courage. Begin to put your courage to work. Start today by knowing that you are capable of meeting all adversities and can rise victorious over every situation. Let the Christ within you take charge of your life and affairs. Give all your fears and worries into His keeping.

Have you lost sight of your courage? You will find it again as you exercise anew your faith and fortitude. Courage is only one of the many facets of faith; it is the expression of one whose life is centered in the certitude, love, and strength of Divine mind. God knows no compromise with fear, worry, or sickness; and God has given you power over all false beliefs. This knowledge results in confidence. *"In quietness and confidence shall be thy strength"* is the promise.

Can you think of God or Practice His Presence without feeling peace? Can any fearful or disturbing thing occur in His Presence? Can you come into His Consciousness without coming into peace? It doesn't matter who you are, or where you are, or what your circumstances are, you have that peace now. It is in you — waiting to be released. Out of peace comes poise, out of poise comes power, and out of power comes plenty. Would you be absolutely fearless? Then you must have His Peace. God is everywhere equally present, but you can only know that which you are. You can only have that which you are. Your fear has already begun to disappear if you have taken the first step toward realizing His Presence. The Law says that "As a man thinketh in his heart, so is he." The thought that really produces results is the thought that emanates from a consciousness of God's Presence.

Jesus said, *"Whosoever shall not receive the kingdom of God as a little child shall in no wise enter therein."* One of the characteristics of the child is his trust. This childish instinct is fostered by the loving care of those to whom he is near and dear.

So it is with the man who seeks courage. While he draws upon the Power within himself, he recognizes the Source of that Power. The Father-Son relationship so beautifully presented in the New Testament can be exemplified in our own lives if we are "meek and lowly in heart," and can say with understanding:

> "I can of mine own self do nothing."

> "All things that the Father hath are mind."

> "Every good gift and every perfect gift is from above and cometh down from the Father of lights, with whom is no variables, neither shadow of turning."

> "I and my Father are one."

The student who has learned through experience the power of meditation has probably learned also how helpful the study of words can be in focusing his attention and illuminating his understanding. The opportunity to follow and enrich a line of thought is unlimited. With the Bible, a concordance, and a dictionary at hand, the student who grows through this approach can ask for nothing but time in which to pursue his study.

Words take on significance and power even while they are held in thought. The word, courage is interesting. The root word is *cor,* meaning heart. Other words from this same root are *accord, chord, cordial,* and *creed.*

We make many uses of the word heart in our daily speech. We say, "She has given her heart away," assuming the heart to be the center of the emotion. The teacher directs the child to learn a passage "by heart," implying that the heart is delegated to handle an important phase of the intellect—memory. The man who has "lost heart" in an emergency we recognize as one who has lost courage. Metaphysicians commonly use heart synonymously with *subconscious mind.*

The specific use of the root word in *courage*, however, gives us this definition: Courage is that firmness of spirit which meets danger without fear.

Perhaps in your need, you will find among the verses that follow a spring-board which will help you take off into that desired area in which there is no fear, in which courage is man's natural state.

> *"Fear not, little flock, it is your Father's good pleasure to give you the kingdom."*
>
> *"Life up thine heart."*
>
> *"Let no man's heart fail him because of him* [the Philistine — that is, the enemy].*"*
>
> *"Keep thy heart* [subconscious mind] *with all diligence; for out of it are the issues of life."*
>
> *"Let the words of my mouth, and the meditation of my heart be acceptable in they sight, O Lord, my strength and redeemer."*
>
> *"The Lord is my strength and my shield; my heart trusted in him, and I am helped; therefore my heart greatly rejoiceth; and with my song will I praise him. The Lord is their strength, and he is the saving grace of the annointed."*

In the American* translation of the Bible these words are set in a rhythmic pattern:

> *The Lord is my strength and my shield; in him my heart has trusted;*
>
> *And I have been helped and my heart exults, and with my song I praise him.*

---

* American Standard Version--Thomas Nelson & Sons.

The Lord is the strength of his people and a refuge; the help of the annointed is be.

The Moffatt[*] translation of the Bible introduces a new figure:

"The Eternal is my strength and shield, my heart has faith in him;

So I am helped, my heart exults, and I sing to his praise.

to the Eternal, the strength of his people, a saving stronghold for his chosen."

"Let not your heart be troubled."

---

[*] A New Translation, James Moffatt, Harper & Brothers Publishers.

Acknowledgments

Any author finds himself under obligation to many persons who do not receive formal credit. There are those to whom he is indebted for ideas; and there are others whose words are remembered when their source is forgotten or impossible to identify. The appreciation of the author is no less sincere because of the impossibility of publicly recognizing their individual assistance.

In the belief bibliography that follows, the author wishes to acknowledge with deep gratitude his use of specific quotations of some length.

CHAPTER I. THE KEY

Pardue, Austin. Your Morale. Charles Scribner's Sons. Used by permission of the author.

CHAPTER III. FEAR—HOW IT WORKS

Southard, Dr. C. O. Truth Ideas of an M. D. Unity of School of Christianity.

CHAPTER IV. FEAR—WHAT IT DOES

Duhamel, Maurice. We Are Not Afraid. Penn Publishing Co.

Larson, Christian D. How To Stay Well. Used by permission of the author.

CHAPTER VI. FEAR—HOW TO MEET IT

Larson, Christian D. How To Stay Well. Used by permission of the author.

Books by Robert A. Russell

You Try It

You, Too, Can Be Prosperous

Putting the Prosperity Idea to Work*

Talk Yourself Out of It

Talk Yourself Into It

In Spite of Everything*

All Things Made New

Vital Points in Demonstration

Victory Over Fear and Worry

You Can Get What You Want If You Find It Within Yourself

God Works Through Silence

God Works Through Faith

God Works Through You (in preparation)

The Answer Will Come

Making the Contact

Dry Those Tears

---

* Temporarily out of print.

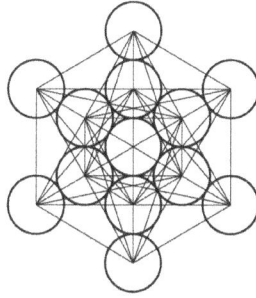

Raisa - Mystic Alchemist

Energy Healing, Chakra Alignment, Sacred Geometry, Sound Healing

Tammy:
I was blessed with a healing session by Raisa last week. She felt like a friend and like-minded gentle soul with comforting Mother Mary essence pouring through her words. Raisa was so in-tuned to my blocks and traumas held within my field. She used her connection to ascended masters I've resonated with such as Yeshua, Mother Mary, Mary Magdalene, Lady Vesta & Amethyst and archangels Metatron, Michael and others to help clear these.

I was able to address childhood trauma situations to flip the stuck energy I've held onto over the years. She also picked up on a few traumatic past-life scenes that have affected my current life. I am an intuitive energy healer who truly felt the shift and healing within. I now feel so much lighter and have clarity regarding my path.

So much love and gratitude to you both, Raisa and Barry for presenting her to my world! (More Testimonials on following Pages)

Contact Raisa to book an Energy Healing
or Chakra Alignment session:
www.RaisinYourIsness.com
raisinyourisness@hotmail.com

Shannon:

This BEAUTIFUL sister...our Raisa... is a treasure beyond compare! After my experience in my personal session with Raisa... the ABSOLUTE confirmation I received, that could ONLY be confirmed by HER mind you... this session solidified EVERYTHING for me. I KNOW that this sister... she is a formidable, magnificent & IRREPLACEABLE component in this Earth plane story we all are invested in! IF YOU ARE DRAWN TO HER FOLLOW YOUR HEART

No other can do what SHE is gifted to do for YOU... YES YOU!

I LOVE YOU dear sister! I am forever grateful for what only you could do and DID for me! I would have happily paid any price for what you gave me! I URGE YOU ALL to schedule a session with this beloved one!

P.S. thank you Barry for sharing her with us all!

∞

Natasha:

I would like to thank Barry for introducing us to Raisa. I have had 2 consultations with her in the last month and I am in total awe of what transpired. Raisa is such a beautiful caring soul! She connected with me as though she has known me forever. Her love and dedication in assisting others is so touching. I had an amazing experience and some profound healing. I received a message from Jeshua which brought tears to my eyes. I could feel the LOVE in the message that was given to me and I will remember and cherish His message forever. Raisa has really helped me in confronting fears, trauma and past life karma. I have found the reason for my skin problems which I never would have thought it'd be possible. It is amazing what guilt and shame from past lives can actually do to your body. Her healing and that from our Angelic beings has really made a huge difference in my life. I can feel it in my energy. Raisa has a lovely sense of humour, always reminding you not to take life and yourself so seriously. I really feel like a heavy weight has been lifted off my soul. Thank you so much! Much Love!

∞

Ariel:

Raisa... Divine Raisa... You are a Treasure to this Life, and I thank All That Is, and this also Treasured YT channel for the priceless blessing which was our session this AM. Every moment of the session was a fractal explosion of wonderful intuitive & divinely guided perfection. I honor your sincere, caring, graceful, playful, soothing, encouraging, transformational, empowering, and so beautiful demonstration / embodiment of Goddess energy and presence. I am so honored & thankful to have been guided to You. To have invested in the patience, time, energy, and resources to share sacred healing and uplifting time with You. I will remember the session Always. And I will look forward to any and all ways our Creator deems it harmonious to connect again. I could go on and on and on, so please accept my parting acknowledgment of your blessing to this realm, my Heart & Spirt, my Life, and the Lives of all those who may be positively impacted via your assistance. Blessings, and Gratitude, a thousand times over and over again. Namaste... Namaste... Namaste...

∞

B.G.

I have just finished a healing session with Raisa. The experience was remarkable! I am still buzzing! I heard about her from this channel, so thank you deeply Barry!

Raisa is so lovely to talk to, and intuitively guided, knows how to get to the hidden roots of our issues. She calls upon ascended masters, archangels and such to do deep energetic clearing and healing work. It was like being guided through the deep layers of myself, releasing the things that don't serve me and filling every cell with light. I purged, and I absorbed new energy, and came out feeling uplifted and renewed. Raisa helped me to find things in myself that I had been cut off from, and to heal wounds I had tried to bury. She has also given me helpful ideas to continue to improve things my life.

I am so blessed to have found Raisa, and ever grateful for the healing work she has done. She is as authentic as they come. Truly an earth angel! Thank you, thank you, thank you!

YouTube

YouTube Channels of Interest:

Giving Voice to the Wisdom of the Ages

Over 5,000 audios, hundreds of
Spiritual and Metaphysical
audio books including
Robert A Russell, Dr Murdo MacDonald Bayne,
Napoleon Hill, Jeshua, Kryon and many more.

I AM Meditations and Affirmations

Hundreds of I AM Meditations,
Daily affirmations and more.

Raisin' Your Isness

Metaphysical Musings, Channelings,
Sound Healing Songs

www.ingramcontent.com/pod-product-compliance
Lightning Source LLC
Chambersburg PA
CBHW021343090426
42742CB00008B/724

About the Author

George A. Goens, Ph.D. is a prominent author, dynamic leader, recognized educator, and featured speaker. George has worked with public and private sector organizations on leadership development, and assessment, and has presented seminars and workshops on leadership and educational reform for regional, state, and national organizations and for school districts across the country.

He published five books: *Mastering School Reform* [Allyn and Bacon], *Getting the Most from Public Schools: A Parent's Guide* [Pineapple Press], *Soft Leadership for Hard Times* [Rowman & Littlefield, 2005], *Leadership for Turbulent Times* [Rowman & Littlefield, 2010], and *Letters on the Promise of Living* [CreateSpace, 2012]. In addition, he has published over 60 articles in national and state periodicals.

Visit him at *www.georgegoens.com*.